THE AMERICAN PILGRIMAGE

CYCLONE COVEY

THE

AMERICAN PILGRIMAGE

The Roots of
American History,
Religion and Culture

but they knew they were pilgrimes, &
... lift vp their eyes to the heauens,
their dearest cuntrie ....
—*William Bradford*

COLLIER BOOKS
NEW YORK, N.Y.

A Collier Books Original

Collier Books is a division of The Crowell-Collier
Publishing Company.

First Edition 1961.

Library of Congress Catalog Card Number: 61-17490.

Contents

Preface

Now what is history? It is the centuries of systematic explorations of the riddle of death, with a view to overcoming death.
—BORIS PASTERNAK, *Doctor Zhivago*, 1958

THE FORGING of the basic American tradition occurred largely at the hands of people whose orienting world-view and fierce motivation was that of a symbolic pilgrimage through the wilderness of this world to an ultimate home town in the next.

Defection from such an allegiance was constant from the first, and some groups never subscribed to it at all; but it held with sufficient strength for 150 years to give colonial thought much of its context, its cast, and its coherence. Though the concept would have been foreign to no denomination in that religion-drenched time, it was most typical of the Puritans and Pietists; and their preponderance in early American intellectual history was such that we may justly speak of the period of about 1600-1750 as the *pilgrimage era*—the era when the pilgrim idea went far to determine the lineaments of the culture. The term most felicitously fits southern New England but applies in varying degree to other sections of the seaboard as well, up to northern Maine and all the way down to South Carolina.

The Great Awakening and its aftermath may be taken as the rough terminal boundary of the pilgrimage era proper; for it was in these transition years from "medieval" to "modern" times that Americans generally accepted the wilderness as home. The emotional acclimitization involved in this acceptance marks an epochal switch in viewpoint that hopelessly separates such pious contemporaries as Benjamin Franklin and Jonathan Edwards. It is this reorientation that makes most of colonial America alien to its heirs, who know Franklin as a familiar old friend but feel little sympathy for the hotter-hearted Edwards, whom they think of as cold. The pilgrimage did not end as a molding denominator of American life when Edwards, after a ministry of more than 23 years, lost his pulpit, and Franklin, having retired from a successful business career, won his first election—two events that closely coincided. But American culture thereafter was more characterizable by those who read Poor Richard's hints on how to succeed in this world than by those who heeded Edwards's *Christian Pilgrim* on how to succeed in the other.

While the old pilgrimage continued to be decisive among certain individuals and groups all through the 19th century and beyond, it ceased to characterize American culture broadly, as before. The Great Awakening did awaken, did conspicuously rejuvenate Puritanism and its underpinning pilgrim allegiance. But it also released pent-up contrary and superseding movements which disclose a widespread revolution in temper. This may have been the biggest revolution in American history.

Yet the habits the pilgrimage had laid down and the gains achieved in its name, or at least in its context, would not likely have disappeared without a trace in the "enlightened" era that outmoded it. Carl Becker went so far as to conclude that the underlying preconceptions of 18th-century thought were still essentially those of the *13th* century, and that men like Jefferson and Franklin "demolished the Heavenly City of St. Augustine only to rebuild it with more up-to-date materials."[1]

The pages that follow present the American pilgrimage as an integrative interpretive vista into our tradition, and as perhaps the most important neglected theme of that tradition. They define the pilgrimage concept, show its actual orienting function, account in some measure for its nature and its hold, illuminate the phenomenon of Puritanism and of pivotal personalities in terms of it, and analyze the steady, and then final drastic break away from it.

THE SMALLNESS of this volume belies the largeness of its indebtedness, and a mere list of benefactors is a hopelessly inadequate acknowledgment, besides being an incomplete list. I nevertheless cordially thank the people and institutions below for furnishing me with source material, valuable information or criticism, or assistance of many kinds which enabled the labor to proceed or proceed better:

Max Savelle, George Rogers Taylor, E. Porter Dickinson, Alton P. Juhlin, Theodore L. Agnew, Richard P. Cecil, Margery Cecil, Bea and Jerome Rubin, Alice Reynolds, Alfred Levin, Robert B. Kamm, Max A. Mitchell, Richard E. Bailey. Marvin T. Edmison, George H. White, Frank E. McFarland, David S. Berkeley, William R. Steckel, Oscar Handlin, Samuel Eliot Morison, Lawrence Gene Lavengood, Beatrice Godwin, John Dustin, Frances King, Anne Hyder, Clifford K. Shipton, Carolyn E. Jakeman, Mary K. Daehler, Julie Johnson, Clarkson A. Collins III, Clifford P. Monahon, Francis L. Berkeley Jr., 2865 Am. Pelgrimage   July 12, '61   Timmerman 2 Roy F. Nichols, Donald C. Holmes, Margaret Scriven, Maurice M. Shudolfsky, Malcolm Freiberg, Paul F. Richards, Stephen T. Riley, Jeannette D. Black, Edward L. Hoffman, Russell Grow, Lewis B. VanWinkle, Stanley Duff Hopper, Stanley Romaine Hopper, Charles Woolsey Cole, Rena Durkan, Robert Freeman Grose, Theodore Phinney Greene, Lois D. Cole, J. Christopher Herold, Esta Wolfram, Gerald W. Eby, Donnell M. Owings, Bruce Ingham Granger, N. Wendell Hansen, Ina A. and Wesley G. Anderson, Mr. and Mrs. D. Conrad Jarvis, Mr. and Mrs. C. D. Covey, and my wife Bonnie;

The Fund for the Advancement of Education, the Carnegie Foundation, the Oklahoma State University Research Foundation, the OSU Arts and Sciences Publication Committee, Reed College, Stanford University, the University of Chicago, the University of Oklahoma, Oklahoma State University, Harvard University, Amherst College, McKendree College and, besides the main libraries of the foregoing institutions, Houghton, Lamont, the Library of Congress, Newberry, Huntington, Alderman, Morgan, Congregational, St. Louis Public, Portland (Ore.) Public, New York Public, Boston Public, Newton Public, West Newton Public, Belleville (Ill.) Public, Union Theological Seminary, Fresno State College, Brown University, John Carter Brown, Yale University, University of Michigan, University of Illinois, University of Wisconsin, University of Kansas, University of Massachusetts, Smith College, and Forbes; Goodspeed's Book Shop, American Antiquarian Society, Harvard Archives, Massachusetts Archives, Massachusetts Historical Society, Rhode Island Historical Society, Chicago Historical Society, Essex Institute, and Recordak Corporation.

Stillwater, Oklahoma
June 1960

Chapter 1

Destination: Death

The goal of all life is death . . . . *Life is but the circuitous route to death.*

> —SIGMUND FREUD, *Beyond the Pleasure Principle,* 1922

. . . . Our whole life is nothing but a race towards death . . . .

> —AURELIUS AUGUSTINE, *The City of God,* 413-26

"As I WALK'D through the wilderness of this world," Bunyan begins *The Pilgrim's Progress,* "I lighted on a certain place, where was a Denn [Bedford Jail]," and there dreamed a dream of the pilgrim, Christian, trudging with a burden on his back to Mount Zion. Christian reads in his book that he must die and come to judgment, but is unwilling to do the first and unable to do the second: He looks as though he would run if he knew which way to go. *"What shall I do to be saved?"* his anguished cry echoes down the centuries—itself re-echoing the question of the Macedonian jailer in *Acts* 16. Jonathan Edwards reports that this was a common cry in the Connecticut Valley early in the Great Awakening.[2] Edwards's father Timothy, on the one occasion of his life when he preached the big election sermon

11

before the Connecticut General Assembly (1732) chose the overriding topic *All the living must surely die, and go to judgment*. Meanwhile, all the living are but pilgrims in a wilderness on their way to a permanent, restful abode in the Celestial City.

The Biblical authority for conceiving the Christian life as a pilgrimage comes from the reinterpretation of Old Testament history in the eleventh chapter of *Hebrews*:

By faith Abraham . . . sojourned in the land of promise, as in a strange country . . . for he looked for a city which hath foundations, whose builder and maker is God.

Abraham and innumerable descendants

all died in faith, not having received the promises, but having seen them afar off, and embraced them, and confessed that they were strangers and pilgrims on the earth. For they that say such things declare plainly that they seek . . . . a better country, that is, a heavenly . . . .

Thus the King James version of 1611. The Wyclif, Tyndale, Cranmer, Geneva, and Rheims versions before it also used the word "pilgrims," whether spelled "pilgryms," "pylgrems," or "pilgrimes."[3] It was this chapter in *Hebrews*—doubtless the Geneva version of 1557—that William Bradford cited in a marginal note when he chronicled the departure of the America-bound Pilgrims from Leyden:

So they lefte that goodly, & Pleasant citie, which had been ther resting place, nere .12. years; but they knew they were pilgrimes, & looked not much on these things; but lift vp their eyes to the heauens, their dearest cuntrie; and quieted their spirits.[4]

Bradford refers to himself personally as a pilgrim in a poem he composed in his last years:

> *In fears and wants, through weal and woe,*
> *A pilgrim, past I to and fro. . . .*[5]

The child born to Mrs. William White on the *Mayflower* in Provincetown Harbor was named Peregrine, a synonym for "pilgrim." The reason the Pilgrims called themselves pilgrims is not that they made a long trip to a wilderness, but that they regarded every moment of their lives as part of a trip to Zion.

They had been exiles in Holland, but their whole earthly tenure, wherever, was to them an exile in a wilderness.

It may not need explaining that Zion was the hill in Jerusalem which David stormed and whereon he established his capital, his palace, and the altar of Israel. In the wilderness the Israelites had called their place of worship the Tabernacle; atop Zion it became the Temple and, for Christians, symbolized the gateway to the Celestial City. Here was the point of contact, in Hebrew tradition, between God and His chosen people. With the New Testament is came also to represent the Church (and so Augustine defines "Tabernacle"), the only portal through which God's people could gain salvation. Hence the pilgrimage must culminate at God's house on earth, the highest one may get in this life; but through it as the gate, one ascends to God's house in heaven. The existence of an actual Zion Gate facilitated the symbolism.

The westward journey of Abraham and his progeny complicates this Zion imagery; for the unknown author of *Hebrews* saw the crossing of the River Jordan into the Promised Land as the after-death ascent into the heavenly country—the crossing of the bar, or boundary between this world and the next. The Puritans in particular regarded Israel, also Zion and Jordan, as "types" prefiguring the New Testament. To them Massachusetts could be as much an Israel as Israel had been, and so they called it. Increase Mather more strictly defined "Israel" (which Augustine points out meant "seeing God") as "the Lords Covenant People," with New England Congregationalists in mind.[6] Puritan Zionism had no commitment to any geographical locus.

John Bunyan found he had to shift the site of his House Beautiful from Zion to another eminence; otherwise, the pilgrim would have to cross Jordan before he could enter the church. While thinking of themselves as in transit and in the church, the American Puritans and sectarians also thought of themselves as Israelites already planted, with their churches, on the summit of Zion. At least, they thought of themselves as replicas of the Israelites; they never really confused their American Zion with the height they ultimately hoped to scale.

The pilgrimage, in summary, signified an inner quest of the Christian within a church context involving a mystical crossing of Jordan at death and an ascent up Zion to see God on His throne in His City and join Him there for eternity. The whole of a Christian's life was conceived to be an up-hill struggle. Jonathan Edwards says in his *Christian Pilgrim* that those who lead holy lives journey through a wilderness with much labor and toil towards heaven, "up the hill toward Zion, against the inclinations and tendency of the flesh . . . ."

This world was made for a place of preparation for another. Man's mortal life was given him, that he might be prepared for his fixed state.[7]

To GO BACK even before *Hebrews* in the western tradition, we find the pilgrimage idea already fully developed by the beginning of the 4th century B. C. (To go back many centuries before Plato in the *eastern* tradition, we find the philosophical poets of India already regarding everyman as a pilgrim [*śramana*] wandering, or disciplining himself, through the stages of his life along the sacred Way to the "farther shore" or celestial strand of the river of life. They also liken this spiritual pilgrimage to the smoke from an altar that ascends to the eye of the dome; so one seeks to ascend through the eye of the dome of heaven; and to die is to "become one" with God.) In Plato's *Phaedo* Socrates talks of the soul's internal pilgrimage, first returning into itself and reflecting, then passing into "the realm of purity, and eternity, and immortality, and unchangeableness"; where it ceases from its erring ways, "and being in communion with the unchanging is unchanging." This state of the soul Plato calls wisdom and equates with virtue.

The philosopher growing in virtue prepares his soul for a more propitious after-death pilgrimage. Anticipating the hemlock, Socrates says that "as I am going to another place, I ought to be thinking and talking of the nature of the pilgrimage which I am about to make." What he meant by "pilgrimage" here was the journey of the soul to the other world after death, a journey involving many partings of the road and many wanderings. Those, he says, who have led holy lives purified by philosophy go to their home above and dwell in mansions "fairer far than these."

Then there is the return pilgrimage of the soul back into life, described in the Myth of Er which concludes the *Republic*. This pilgrimage in reverse culminates with the crossing of Lethe, the River of Forgetfulness, which brings the soul back into earthly life, as in Bunyan the crossing of Jordan brings the soul into everlasting life. While rejecting Plato's belief in transmigration of souls and in partial recollection of a previous state, Christianity retains a counterpart longing to go home and to recall the perfect vision clouded since the Fall.

Plato immediately concerns himself, however, with the earthly pilgrimage—the aspiration via reason divorced from the senses to grasp "essential reality," "the very nature of Goodness itself." This journey, the "travelling up to the first principle of all," "the passion to see the truth," Plato calls Dialectic.[8]

Plotinus, the main link between Plato and Augustine, defines "dialectic" as "the Upward Way." The mounting wayfarer, says Plotinus, is a godlike man, one who has "clear vision of the splendor above," toward which he rises from the cloud and fog of earth. Looking beyond all here, he delights in that other world, "the place of reality," his "native land,"

like a man returning after long wanderings to the pleasant ways of his own country.[9]

Augustine, who freely admits that his conversion to Christianity came by way of the Platonists, resumes the question-and-answer technique of Plato's dialectic (as adapted in Latin by Cicero) in his *Soliloquies*. He calls this scholarly-conversational pursuit the "going to God" or the virtue "whereby we journey"; in his *Sermon 92* he defines God as "the home whither we go" and "the way whereby we go." The Church, he says in his *Tractate on John*, knows two lives divinely preached and commended unto her:

one is in the time of pilgrimage, the other in eternity of abiding; the one is in labor, the other in rest; the one is on the way, the other in the [true] country . . . .[10]

The real theme of the first two books of his great treatise, *On Christian Doctrine*, is the pilgrimage. Suppose, says Augustine, that we were wanderers in a strange country feeling wretched away from our fatherland and, to put an end to our misery, determined to return home, but that the beauty of the countryside and the very pleasure of our motion diverted our thoughts from what would make us truly happy. So we have wandered far from God and, if we wish to return to our Father's home, the soul must be purified so it can discriminate clearly the invisible things of our Father's country—use this world but not enjoy it. "And let us look upon this purification as a kind of journey or voyage to our native land." The more we enjoy Him in this life as through a glass darkly, the more easily we are able to bear our pilgrimage and the more eagerly we long for its termination. It is while one wanders as a stranger in the world and fixes his affections entirely upon the future unchangeable life that he is in his optimum state; and the way he takes is "not a way through space, but through a change of affections."[11]

The pilgrimage also becomes a theme of certain parts of Augustine's long, trenchant classic, *The City of God.* Book XIX, chapter 17 makes the most use of the pilgrimage figure and most fully recapitulates the concept. From the beginning of the work as a whole, however, Augustine is distinguishing between the earthly city that lives according to men, and the heavenly that is mingled with it but lives according to God. The citizen of the latter "is as yet a pilgrim journeying on to the celestial city" which is eternal. The desire for that promised, peaceful habitation is what draws the Christian on, through faith, "in this miserable pilgrimage." By bearing one another's burdens and growing in grace, "the citizens of the city of God are healed while still they sojourn in this earth and sigh for the peace of their heavenly country." In this world, in these evil days, from the time of Abel and thenceforth even to the end of this world, "the Church has gone forward on pilgrimage amid the persecutions of the world and the consolations of God."[12] Augustine's City of God is therefore the Pilgrim City.

Now the Puritans were before everything else Augustinian,[13] though they are commonly called Calvinist. But Calvin was also before everything else Augustinian. In his monumental systematic theology Calvin repeated that "while we are aspiring towards our true country, we be pilgrims on earth."[14] His *Catechism* underscores that

our happiness is not located on earth . . . . we are to live in this world as foreigners, thinking continually of departure, and not allowing our hearts to be involved in earthly delights.[15]

Calvin's sermons return to the theme; for instance, one on 2 *Timothy* 2. 16-18:

' We must learn to . . . walk fearfully and carefully . . . . St. Paul hath shown us, that . . . we must walk in death before we can come to life. How long will this death continue? As long as we are in this world . . . . Until God shall take us out of this world, we must be as pilgrims in a strange country . . . .[16]

Dante opens his *Commedia* "in the middle of the journey" of his life, having strayed from the way. When he comes to his senses, he tries to proceed on uphill toward on a mountain but has not the strength to overcome the temptations of this world. The mountain he is trying to scale is Zion, which turns out to be the same as Mount Purgatory. He cannot negotiate it directly but must go down through hell first, at length gaining the Mountain's summit from within, crossing "the sacred river" (Lethe), and ascending, escorted, to the realm of peace and light.

Shakespeare has Richard II unfeelingly intone the pilgrim concept on the death of Lancaster: "His time is spent, our pilgrimage must be." Francis Bacon invokes it contritely in April 1621: "my soul hath been a stranger in the course of my pilgrimage." Sir Walter Raleigh, beneath his taciturnity, clasps it:

> *Give me my scallop-shell of quiet,*
> *My staff of faith to walk upon.*
> *My scrip of joy, immortal diet,*
> *My bottle of salvation,*
> *My gown of glory, hope's true gage;*
> *And thus I'll take my pilgrimage. . . .*
>
> *Whilst my soul, like quiet palmer,*
> *Travelleth towards the land of heaven;*
> *Over the silver mountains. . . .*

But this is an age-old idea, found fully formed in antiquity and in familiar usage in western Europe at least from the 12th century. One of its most striking restatements in England in the period of the first colonizing of New England occurs in a funeral sermon that John Taylor delivered in 1622 or earlier, entitled *The Pilgrims Profession*. Taylor was a disciple of the Cambridge professor, William Perkins, who decisively influenced John Cotton, among countless others. Taylor took for his text on this occasion one that Increase Mather later made much of: "I am a stranger with thee, and a sojourner," from Psalm 39. The carriage (deportment) of the saint through this life,

Taylor said, is like that of the traveler going home through a strange country, bearing the three-fold burden of sin, worldly care, and fear of death.

Hee will through thicke and thin, through drops and drout and all because he is going home . . . . Now how happily shall this man compasse his journey and goe singing through the most tedious wayes of his Pilgrimage that hath . . . furnished himselfe with the understanding of the way . . . .[17]

JOHN WINTHROP, the most influential political figure of first-generation Massachusetts, had long been a pilgrim when he won the 1629 election in London as governor of the Bay Company. Back in March or April 1618, a few weeks before his marriage to Margaret Tyndal, he bade her let worldly minds that savor not the things of God bend all their care and study to secure themselves an earthly happiness.

But you, whom God hathe ordayned to a better ende, he lookes you should be guided by an other rule; he telles you that you are a pilgrime & stranger in this life, that you have no abidinge cytye heere but must looke for one to come . . .

In the black-looking spring of 1629, on April 28, he wrote her from London that he trusted God's mercy "to carry us along through this course of our pilgrimage, in the peace of a good conscience . . . ."[18]

John Winthrop Jr. had sojourned to Constantinople and had participated in the British naval failure to relieve the Huguenots at La Rochelle when he wrote his father rather world-wearily 21 August 1629 about embarking for New England:

I have seene so much of the vanity of the world that I esteeme noe more of the diversities of Countries then as so many Innes, wherof the travailer, that hath lodged in the best, or in the worst findeth noe difference when he commeth to his Journies end . . . .[19]

The Roxbury minister Thomas Welde, in his preface to Winthrop Sr.'s account of the Antinomian convulsion, published 1644, observes that "our wise God . . . seldome suffers his owne, in this their wearysome Pilgrimage to be long without trouble . . . ."[20]

"The city where I hope to dwell," says another first-generation Puritan, Ann Bradstreet, "There's none on earth can parallel . . . ." This in her poem of 1678, *The Flesh and the Spirit.*

> *If I of Heaven may have my fill,*
> *Take thou the world, and all that will.*

She follows the time-honored custom of referring to her pilgrimage as "weary." One of her poems (dated 31 August 1669) bears the actual title *A Pilgrim* and goes in part:

> *A Pilgrim I on Earth, perplext,*
> *With sins with cares and sorrows vext.*[21]

Roger Williams sounds Bunyanesque in 1672, six years before Bunyan's classic, when he says that we wilfully stumble into the Ditch Eternal by refusing the word of Scripture, which is a light to our feet and lantern to our paths. "Thus the Heavenly Sun-Dial is one and constant in its guidance and direction to us poor Travellers."[22]

Williams's local enemy William Harris refers to himself in a petition to the king 11 June 1675 as "A weary traueller for the Space of almoste forty years In the wildernes of New England . . . ."[23]

Increase Mather, the leading Puritan during the last quarter of the 17th century, talks in his old age of "the dayes of my pilgrimage now drawing to their close";[24] he speaks of his wife as "the Dear Companion of my Pilgrimage on Earth,"[25] and of the years that his and his son's lives overlapped as "Our Peregrination together thro' the Wilderness."[26] To one of his funeral sermons he appends a coda-section: "Meditations on death, and on the heavenly-countrey which believers go into at the hour of death," on the text: "For we are Strangers before thee, and Sojourners, as were all our Fathers: Our Dayes on the Earth are as a Shadow, and there is none abiding."[27]

Solomon Stoddard, who dominated Connecticut-Valley Puritanism as Increase Mather did that of the seaboard in their time, designed his 1714 *Guide to Christ* mostly, he says on the title page, for young ministers and partly for private Christians "who are enquiring the way to Zion."

When Cotton Mather, the dominant Puritan of the gener-

ation between Increase's and Edwards's, called himself a
"Fellow Traveller" and addressed his readers: "O my *Fellow
Travellers*," no one would mistake that he meant pilgrims "to
that Glorius World." He characteristically calls it "the *Heavenly World*" rather than the more customary Heavenly Country
or Celestial City, but it is the identical destination.

> Look upwards, and you shall soon say . . . . *We faint not,
> while we look to the Things that are not seen.* Look and see there
> what you have to encourage you under the Difficulties of your
> *Pilgrimage.*[28]

In his autobiography Cotton Mather epitomizes his life as a
"poor *walk with god*."[29] In *Coheleth* he speaks of himself as
"Hastening to the *Conclusion* of my *Pilgrimage,* thro' *this
present Evil World* . . . . while you [*my Son*] are yet . . . . no
further from the *Beginning* of your *Pilgrimage* . . . ."[30] In his
metaphorical *Agricola* he inserts a poem between chapters entitled "The Plain Songs of the Pious Husbandman; In the *Work*
of his *Husbandry*, and the *House* of his *Pilgrimage*."[31]

The polished Boston minister, Benjamin Colman, who knew
both Cotton Mather and Edwards, advised young ministers in
his funeral sermon for Stoddard in 1729 not to "count upon
attaining the Days of the Years of their Pilgrimage. . . ."[32] John
Dickinson, an anti-Great-Awakening minister at Elizabethtown,
New Jersey, recapitulated the pilgrim concept as the orientation
of the Christian life at even greater length than Edwards's
Christian Pilgrim.[33] In the same year as Dickinson's work
(1745), a collection of poems by Cotton Mather's young
disciple, John Adams, a minister living at Cambridge, came to
print posthumously in Boston. It included lines extolling divine
grace, a force, says Adams.

> *Which broke my Soul from all its servile Chains,
> And fix'd my Feet on* Zion's *wid'ning Plains.*[34]

THE OTHERWORDLY DESTINATION of the pilgrimage explains
why Puritans focally emphasized death, even as the 2nd-century
church father Irenaeus had said: "The business of the Christian
is nothing else than to be ever preparing for death."[35] "Do you
not know," Paul wrote the Romans, "that all of us who have
been baptized into Christ Jesus were baptized into his death?"

Long before Christ, Socrates had said (according to Plato's *Phaedo*) that other men do not perceive that the true disciple of philosophy "is ever pursuing death and dying." This disciple, says Socrates, has reason to be of good cheer when about to die, for "after death he may hope to receive the greatest good in the other world." "Men see Him just so far as they die to this world," says Augustine (*On Christian Doctrine,* II. 7). Augustine chides his friend Nebridius in a letter of 389 for wanting him to make the long journey for a visit:

To go through life planning journeys that cannot be undertaken without disturbance and trouble does not become one who is planning for that last journey we call death; with it alone, as you are aware, should our real plans be concerned.[36]

Montaigne reaffirms this whole set of traditional views in his famous essay, *That to study philosophy is to learn to die.*

Cotton Mather said 1726: "the Contemplation of DEATH shall be the FIRST Point of the *Wisdom* that my Advice must lead you to." As the leading Puritan of the entire first quarter of the 18th century, he was giving his final advice to ministerial candidates who would soon assume the burden of maintaining Puritanism.

Place yourself in the *Circumstances* of a *Dying Person;* your Breth failing, your *Throat* rattling, your *Eyes* with a dim Cloud, and your *Heads* with a damp Sweat upon them: And *then* entertain such Sentiments of *this World,* and of the *Work* to be done in this World, that such a *View* must needs inspire you withal.[37]

"So teach us to number our Days, that we may apply our Hearts to Wisdom." Mather quotes Psalm 90 for a sermon, *Death Made Happy,* published in London in 1701. God, he says, seems to entertain many of us with a handwriting somewhat like that which terrified Belshazzar of old. It should stir us. "to renounce this *World,* the *Flesh,* and the *Devil . . . .*"[38] Mather comes directly to grips with the pilgrim theme in a companion discourse, *Death Made Easie,* on the text from Psalm 119.19, "I am a Stranger in the Earth":

It is usually the delirious, but the observable Fancy of *Dying Men, That they are not at Home.* And yet it would be . . . the highest *Reasonableness,* in every Man *living,* to count himself, *not at Home,* until he dies . . . . Yea, let a Man *live* like a *Stranger* in this, and that Man shall *die* as a *Citizen* of another, and a better World . . . . The Life of *a Stranger in the World,* is that which all the servants of God have evermore espoused; it is the *Epitaph* which the Spirit of God has at last inscribed upon their Tombs, in *Heb.* 11. 13. *These dyed in Faith and confess that they were Strangers and Pilgrims on the Earth . . . .*[39]

"Let your *Meditations* upon your Death be solemn, serious, and very frequent," Mather says in the last discourse of this trilogy, *Serious Thoughts in Dying Times.*

THE THOUGHTS of DEATH, are *at all Times* too *seasonable,* and too *profitable,* to be *justly* laid aside; were our Deaths more considered, our Lives would be more circumspect, serious, gracious; and if the *Contemplation of Death,* were with any Reason of old assigned as the Great *Exercise* of true *Philosophy,* it may much more be accounted the Grand Incentive of right *Christianity . . . .*[40]

Mather explains the mystery (though a mystery only to moderns) of why the autocratic Salem Puritan, John Endecott, should have sealed all his letters with a skull: "That Man is like to die comfortably," says Mather, "who is every Day minding himself, that he is to die shortly. Let us look upon every thing as a short of *Death's-Head* set before us, with a *Memento mortis* written upon it."[41] This view had been a late-medieval commonplace.

And what was the nature of this death that should preoccupy one's mind in life? In the Celestial City, Augustine thought, the soul would enjoy eternal and perpetual Sabbath. The Christian doctrine of the re-creation and resurrection of a new body identical to the distintegrating one proved something of an embarrassment to the Platonic notion of the immortality of the soul alone and unfettered. Like Augustine, Cotton Mather tended to ignore the corporeal side of the afterlife. Yet he thought that some matter from the head served as a vehicle to convey the spirit away from the body.[42] Like Luther, among others, Mather fell back on the metaphor of sleep in conceiving of death.

Death to the Faithful, is a SLEEP . . . . The Great Thing to be now pressed upon us all, is this. *Make due provision for it,* That when you *Dy,* you may *Sleep Comfortably.*[43]

Fifteen years later, in his last sermon, Mather returned to the question of the sleep of death which the saint has made sure will be without bad dreams.

'Tis indeed a *Rest* . . . . And yet the chief sweet of the *rest,* is that it is *without rest.* It is a *rest* from *irksome* and *vexing* things; Not a *rest* from the *joyful praises* of God . . . . The *spirits* of them who *sleep* in *Jesus* are not lull'd into *sleep* of utter *inactivity* and *insensibility there.* How the disengaged *spirits* of good men exert their operations, who can tell . . . .[44]

Mather had done most of his speculating back before the turn of the century on what God has in store at the climactic moment of dissolution:

Let us Believe ,that He has Legions and Myriads, and Millions of Blessed *Spirits*, to be our Convoy, and afeguard from those *Evil Spirits*, which are waiting to arrest our *Spirits* . . . .

Thousands of angels from God's Holy Place will "fly like swift Flashes of Lightning to succour us . . . ." But whoever is without the Grant of Grace will be doomed unto Outer Darkness.[45]

"Oh long for the harvest, long for your departure, and for *the appearing of Christ,*" Cotton's grandfather, Richard Mather, said in his farewell address to his congregation at Dorchester (six miles south of Boston) in 1657.[46] Richard's contemporary, John Robinson, the pastor of the Pilgrims in Leyden, said in his 1625 essay *Of Death* that we should not live "in a senseless blockishness, overcoming death, as the most do, by forgetting it; as if a man overcame his enemy, by getting as far from him as he could"; we should instead take occasion by the death of friends "to love this world less . . . and heaven the more . . . ."[47]

The death of the imperious Solomon Stoddard in February 1729 at the age of 86, moved young William Williams, who preached his funeral sermon at Northampton, to enjoin everybody "to *make ready for Death* . . . . This is the great Business of Life . . . ."[48] Colman in his funeral sermon for Stoddard at Boston eleven days after Williams's, concluded that "The *Crown* of Life is to finish well, in *happy Death.* And the way to *this* is to pass our Days here under the governing Tho'ts of Death and *Eternity.*"[49]

Jonathan Edwards, who more than once in his notes alludes

specifically to the City of God, talks as though he had taken all these men's advice. But he was taking it largely from the same traditional sources as they. "Frequently in my Pursuits of whatever Kind," Edwards writes in his diary, "let this come into my Mind; 'How much shall I value this on my Death Bed?' "[50] His ninth resolution says: "Resolved, to think much on all Occasions of my own dying, and of the Common Circumstances which attend Death."[51] And why? "To obtain for myself as much happiness, in the other world, as I possibly can."[52]

In his culminative sermon, *The Christian Pilgrim*, he elaborates:

> Our whole lives ought to be spent in travelling this road. We ought to begin *early*. This should be the *first* concern, when persons become capable of acting. When they first set out in the *world*, they should set out on *this* journey. And we ought to travel with *assiduity*. It ought to be the work of every day. We should often think of our journey's end; and make it our daily work to travel on in the way that leads to it. He who is on a journey, is often thinking of the destined place; and it is his daily care and business to get along; and to improve his time to get towards his journey's end. Thus should heaven be continually in our thoughts; and the immediate entrance or passage to it, *viz.* death, should be present with us . . . . All other concerns of life, ought to be entirely subordinate to this.[53]

But to turn to that impetuous Puritan preacher whom the "orthodox" Puritans banished from Massachusetts, the rigid Separatist and radical democrat, Roger Williams. Did *he* regard himself a pilgrim who should be thinking constantly about death? Ah. listen. Let us, he tells his wife, "live the rest of your *short uncertaine span,* more as *strangers*, longing and breathing after another *Home* and *Country* . . . ." It is of "great and sweet use," says he,

> daily to thinke each day our *last,* the day of our last *farewell* . . . . we are but strangers in an *In,* but passengers in a Ship, and though we dreame of long *Summer* dayes, yet our very life and being is but a swift short *passage* from the bank of *time* to the other side or *Banck* of a dolefull *eternity* . . . .[54]

"Eternitie (O Eternitie) is our business," he reminds Governor Simon Bradstreet.[55]

Yes, even a democratic Puritan was still a pilgrim. Williams made a literal pilgrimage through wilderness in deep snow and suffered severe privations before finally founding Providence. When his puzzled old friend Governor Winthrop wrote him, why did he bring this suffering on himself? "To what end do you drive?" Williams replied in the language of the pilgrim, forty years before Bunyan's book: "I aske the way to lost Zion . . . ."[56]

Chapter 2

Plantonic Light, Puritan and Quaker Inner Light, Augustinian Ecstasy, and Puritan Sweet Delight

And yet separation from the world, and so from the men of the world, and so from the prince of the world that reigneth in them, and so from whatsoever is contrary to God, is the first step to our communion with God, and angels, and good men, as the first step to a ladder is to leave the earth!

—JOHN ROBINSON, *An Answer to a Censorious Epistle*, 1608

IN THE PILGRIM'S PROGRESS Bunyan has the Shepherds of the Delectable Mountains conduct Christian and his fellow sojourner Hope to the top of a high hill to look through a "Perspective Glass," and the two pilgrims think they see "something like the Gate, and also some of the Glory" of the Celestial City. When they do later reach the City, amid the sound of trumpets, bells, and angelic choirs, they find that it shines like the sun.

This symbolism of ascent to eternal light——the attempt to glimpse the glory of the hereafter while yet living on earth—typifies an earlier otherworldly tradition as well as the Christian pilgrimage. Plato likens the mass of mankind to prisoners chained in a dark cave who need to be led up into the light. Plato had an almost pathetic longing for permanence and abstract perfection, growing out of a sense of the ephemeral and imperfect character of this world. He speaks of the philosopher as having "a constant passion for any knowledge that will reveal . . . something of that reality which endures for ever and is not always passing into and out of existence." This reality— absolute justice, beauty, and good, and the essence or true nature of everything—cannot be viewed by the eyes or reached with any other bodily sense, "but with the very light of the mind in her clearness, penetrates into the very light of truth in each." Plato does not deviate from the Greek definition of "knowledge" as "union with the Divine." "I cannot think of any study as making the mind look upwards," says Socrates in the *Republic,* "except one which has to do with unseen reality."

Augustine similarly set as the highest aim of man in this life the directing of his soul upward to the Unchanging in order to get a glimpse or foretaste of eternal bliss. This Unchanging he calls Wisdom, Truth, Light, and God. Not shadows but reality, not consequences but the first principle, not sensual pleasures but eternal things. This mind of ours, he says in his *Ennaration of Psalm 41,* seeks a Truth not subject to change, a Substance not capable of failing. In *De Quantitate Animae* he calls this quest the "going to God," in other words, "to the very contemplation of Truth"; and this "striving to grasp intellectually those things which truly and supremely are, is the highest act of seeing of the soul."

As the Celestial City shines like a sun in Bunyan, so in Augustine—who gave currency to the term "Celestial City" in his *City of God*—the "Truth unchangeable shines like a sun in the soul." (Cotton Mather said: "My SOUL is a *Lamp*, shot forth and lit up, immediately from the Glorious God."[57]) Augustine says he followed the Platonists' admonition to return into himself, and retreating into his "inmost self," beheld "with the eye of my soul" above it and his mind, "the Light Unchangeable . . . . He that knows the Truth, knows what that Light is; and he that knows It, knows Eternity, Love knoweth It." In the seventh book of the *Confessions* he describes his inner journey step by step upward whereby his soul abstracted itself from the contradictory throng of sense images and found itself bathed in light, when it knew the Unchangeable; "with the flash of one trembling glance it arrived at THAT WHICH IS."

The Puritan emigrants to America sometimes sound highly reminiscent of Augustine. Thomas Hooker, for instance, says that our Saviour leads us 'by the hand, as it were, to that fountain and first rise of all, and so to the highest step and staire in Heaven which will point at eternity."[58] Hooker's son-in-law Thomas Shepard thought that Heaven on earth consisted in placing *"all my Happiness in being one in and with Christ"*; and but for the sake of others and their good, he adds, "I would meddle no more with this world."[59]

However convincingly Bunyan externalizes it, the pilgrimage is an *internal* upward quest—not through space but through a change of affections, as Augustine says. Plotinus, who devoted his life to this mystic effort to unite with God, sounds already very Augustinian when he says that the heavenly country is reached "in pain of love towards beauty" by taking refuge from material loveliness in things whose beauty is of the soul, and thence rising to the uttermost source of this spiritual loveliness, the First Principle, whose beauty is self-springing. "This attained, there is an end to the pain inassuageable before." The journey is

a going forth from the self, a simplifying, a renunciation, a reach towards contact and at the same time a repose, a meditation towards adjustment . . . . When the soul begins to mount, it comes not to something alien but to its very self; thus detached, it is not in nothingness but in itself . . . it is in the Supreme . . . . If from that heightened self we pass still higher—image to archetype—we have won the Term of all our journeying . . . .

This is the life of gods and of the godlike and blessed among men, liberation from the alien that besets us here, a life taking no pleasure in the things of earth, the passing of solitary to solitary.[60]

Augustine Chritianized the Platonic-Plotinian quest: "though Wisdom was Himself our home, He made Himself also the way by which we should reach our home."[61] The place where the pilgrim seeks the Eternal Wisdom is in His tabernacle on earth, the Church; for it is through the tabernacle that the way lies to the house of God, where is to be found the fountain of understanding. In the *Ennaration of Psalm 41* Augustine interprets that the Psalmist drew near the house of God in going up to the tabernacle, following the leadings of a certain delight, an inward mysterious and hidden pleasure, as if from the house of God there sounded sweetly some instrument; and he, whilst walking in the tabernacle, hearing a certain inward sound, led on by its sweetness, and following the guidance of the sound, withdrawing himself from all the noise of flesh and blood, made his way on even to the house of God . . . .

Here he finds a never-ending festival, the angelic choir making eternal holiday, the presence of God's face generating joy that never fails. From that everlasting festivity

there sounds in the ears of the heart a mysterious strain, melodious and sweet, provided only the world do not drown the sounds. As he walks in this tabernacle . . . the sound of that festivity charms his ears and bears the *hart* away to the *water-brooks*.[62]

JONATHAN EDWARDS *who*, incidentally, brought together a collection of notes under the Platonic-Augustinian title *Shadows of Divine Things,* also frequently uses the word "sweet" in describing his own experience of contemplating or closing with the Divine. This contemplation—and that is the word Augustine uses for it—consisted of "inward struggles and conflicts, and selfreflections" which gradually brought Edwards "a new sense of things." His rather brief *Personal Narrative* that recalls his history of contemplation uses "sweet" or "sweetness" 48 times.

I walked abroad alone, in a solitary Place in my Father's Pasture, for Contemplation. And as I was walking there, and looked up on the Sky and Clouds; there came into my Mind, a sweet Sense of the glorious Majesty and Grace of GOD, that I know not how to express.[63]

God's communication of His Holy Spirit, Edwards says, appeared to him as the pouring forth of divine glory and sweetness from an infinite fountain, "like the sun in its glory, sweetly and pleasantly diffusing light and life." Once in 1737, he says, he caught a view of the glory of God for about an hour, as near as he could judge, which kept him in a flood of tears the greater part of the time. Such contemplation of Holiness brought him to feel it as of "a sweet, pleasant, charming, serene, calm nature." He speaks of "an inward sweetness, that would carry me away, in my contemplations."

This I know not how to express otherwise, than by a calm, sweet abstraction of soul from all the concerns of this world; and sometimes a kind of vision . . . of being alone in the mountains, or some solitary wilderness, far from all mankind, sweetly conversing with Christ, and wrapt and swallowed up in God.[64]

The saintly Governor Winthrop, in his own personal narrative of a hundred years before, says that following a lingering fever at Cambridge University when he was about fourteen, he betook himself to God; but he went through many ups and downs in his inner struggles before it was possible for him to say: "Now could my soule close with Christ, and rest there with sweet content . . . . Now I could goe into any company and not loose him: and so sweet was his love to mee as I desired nothing but him in heaven or earth."[65] Roger Williams concurs: *"Christs consolations* are so sweet, that the soule that tasteth

them in truth, in suffering for any truth of his, will not easily part with them, though thousands are deceiv'd and deluded with counterfeits."[66] Shepard's diary, 9 January 1641:

As I was walking in my Study, musing on my Sermon . . . . I considered. when I come to Christ there is no Wrath or Justice to devour, but sweet Love . . . . It was then objected, But it is to the Elect only. The Lord let me then see, I had nothing to do with that, but to look on his Truth, which is to them that come to him, that he would stand as a Rock between the scorching Sun and their Souls. Hence my Heart was sweetly ravished, and began to long to die, and think of being with him.[67]

"Sweet" (*dulce*), we have seen, was one of Augustine's favorite words to describe the same phenomenon. He speaks of "something melodious and sweet to the ears of the heart," of being "ravished by desire to the inward sweetness of God," "rejoiced by a certain inward sweetness," "fixed with sweet delight in the contemplation of Truth," of "experiences of the sweet life the soul lives when it dies to bodily affections," and of "a wondrous sweetness" in apposition with a foretaste of eternal life. "Thou sweetness never failing. Thou blissful and assured sweetness," he addresses God. To Augustine, as to Plato, Plotinus, Gregory, Bernard, Francis, Bonaventura, Thomas à Kempis, Winthrop, Shepard, Edwards, et al., this mystic ecstasy of merging with the divine was one of calm, peace, and sweetness, even amidst streaming tears.

Augustine told his friend Nebridius that complete withdrawal from the turmoil of transitory things is essential before a man can develop fearlessness in the face of death, and that "that familiarity with death that we are seeking . . . I cannot relish and enjoy . . . unless I obtain release from work and worry." Death is always the point of reference, and Augustine goes on to say that fearlessness in the face of death and the familiarity with it that he is seeking are what comprise "the origin of that solid joy with which no pleasure from any transistory source is in any way to be compared."[68] He elsewhere attempts a definition of the contemplative closure:

> When the attention of the mind is wholly turned away and withdrawn from the bodily senses, it is called an ecstasy . . . . It is a state midway between sleep and death: The soul is rapt in such wise as to be withdrawn from the bodily senses more than in sleep, but less than in death.[69]

So Augustinian ecstasy turns out to be something like the Nirvana of Buddhism or the Wagnerian love-death. (Wagner expressly identifies the love-death with Nirvana.) It sounds like Wordsworth a few miles above Tintern Abbey and Shelley in the *Hymn to Intellectual Beauty,* etc. Augustine and Plato, along with Plotinus, go far to explain the point of Romanticism, including Transcendentalism. Sigmund Freud, whom Lionel Trilling says culminates 19th-century Romantic literature with psychoanalysis, defines his "pleasure-principle" not as the pursuit to repeat sensual indulgence but as a tendency that aims to render the psychic apparatus as a whole *free* from any excitation, at least to keep the excitation constant or as low as possible; which might came close to defining Augustinian ecstasy.

If Freud omits religious longing as the motivation for this state, we know few other Romantics who omitted it, though they rarely called it by that name. Romanticism of the 19th century deliberately obscured its close identity with 17th-century Puritanism by couching its Augustinian religious longing in non-theological terms. Although powerfully feeling the same longing, it had a far more difficult time *believing.* Romanticism, however, retained the term "death," and Freud exhibits the same obsession with it as the 19th-century poets or the 17th-century Puritans.

IN THEIR TALK of solitude and inner light, Augustine and Edwards sound much like Quakers. William Coddington, as a matter of fact, pointed out to the Massachusetts magistrates in 1672 that "God's seed" in the persecutions of the first half of the 17th century in England were "then called *Puritans*," but are "now called *Quakers*," and he quoted the chief spokesman of Bay Puritanism, John Cotton, in favor of moral and against ceremonial Puritans.[70] The wealthy manorial lord, Coddington, who came over in the *Arbella* with Winthrop as a magistrate and who defected with the Antinomians and finally turned Quaker in Rhode Island, illustrates the natural continuity of Quakerism from Puritanism.

To the orthodox Puritans, a deep gulf divided them from the Antinomian and Quaker enthronement of individual intuition and emotion, short-circuiting reason, learning, the Bible, the clergy, and even, in extreme instances, government. Quakerism anticipated the Enlightenment in its simplification of dogma into what is called merely Piety; and the Puritans regarded this trend as further undermining the religious edifice and sanctioning ignorance. Except for a few aristocratic leaders like Coddington and Penn (who successfully kept Quakerism politically conservative), the Quakers came largely from the lower classes and therefore bore a social stigma. In their early sectarian zeal, they obnoxiously disrupted the civil peace and affronted the dignity of government—not merely in refusing to put off their hats in court, in addressing judges with the then-familiar "thee" and "thou," and blurting out imprecations in the form of exasperating sermons in the middle of solemn court proceedings, but in more scandalous ways; as when a comely Quaker housewife walked nude into a Newbury church service, and when some soot-blackened Quaker girls rushed into a Boston church service announcing they had brought the black pox.[71]

Whether the Puritans could see it or not, Quakerism had much in common with Puritanism, including common roots and a common destination. Even Cotton Mather, who was perhaps the first Puritan to speak out publicly against the persecution of Quakers, could admit no kinship with these "madmen," though he noticed that Quakerism had been turning quiet and respectable of late. Coddington was nevertheless not the last Quaker to consider Quakers as the true Puritans of the mid-17th century. William Penn himself made claims in the second half of the 17th century for Quakerism as a return to primitive Christianity that sound like the Puritan claims of the first half. This is the burden, for instance, of his 1672 book, *Quakerism a New Nick-Name for Old Christianity*.[72] In a later book, *Primitive Christianity Revived in the Faith and Practice of the People called Quakers*, he says the Quakers lay down as a main fundamental in religion that God, through Christ, has placed a principle in every man.

> By this *Principle* they understand something that is Divine, and though in Man, *yet not of Man*, but of God; that came from him, and leads to him all those that will be led by it . . . . They call it *the Light of Christ within Man*, or Light within, which is their Ancient and most General and Familiar Phrase . . . . Without [this Principle] there is no *Conviction*, so no *Conversion*, or *Regeneration;* and consequently no entring into the Kingdom of God.[73]

Penn goes on to point out that whereas all men are thus enlightened, they are not all good, because they disobey the light; as all men have reason but are not reasonable. Plato similarly thought all men capable of seeing the light but that only philosophers, who devotedly sought it, saw it.

Besides the light within, Quakers also spoke of the still, small voice within, and so recommended silence and sought solitude, "For nothing reaches the Heart," says Penn, "but what is *from the Heart* . . . ."

> Remember it is a *still Voice*, that speaks to us in this Day, and that is not to be heard in the *Noises* and *Hurries* of the Mind, but is distinctly understood in a *retired Frame*. Jesus *loved* and *chose* Solitudes . . . .[74]

Penn quotes and cites Augustine numerous times toward the end of his climactic work, *No Cross, No Crown* and, at the end of his *Fruits of a Father's Love*, urges his children to read Plato and Plotinus, among other authors. As Augustine followed the advice of the Platonists to be introspective (and found Him "within the very heart"), so Penn advised Quakers: "Love the Truth in your Hearts, be inward to the Lord, that you may grow in the Life and Wisdom of it . . . . and be preserved through the *Noise, Snares* and *Hurry* of this present Evil World."[75] Augustine had spoken of "arriving at a shrine of quiet" and of "a breath of serenity and eternity" and, in the ninth book of the *Confessions,* virtually founded the Quaker position:

If the tumult of the flesh were hushed; hushed the sense impressions of earth, sea, sky . . . hushed all dreams and revelations which come by imagery; if every tongue and every symbol, and all things subject to transiency were wholly hushed . . . . and He alone speak . . . so that we may hear His word . . . may hear His Very Self without intermediary at all—as now we reached forth and with one flash of thought touched the Eternal Wisdom that abides over all . . . .

Augustine exhibits the same confusion as the Quakers as to whether it is a voice heard or a light seen, or something else. "What do I love when I love Thee?" he asks in the tenth book of the *Confessions,* and answers: "a light, melody, fragrance, food, embrace of the inner man." "Light" would be most characteristic of him, as when he describes the contemplative climax as "spiritual contact with the Light unchangeable." And "the light within" would be most characteristic of the Quakers. But the sophisticated attempts at analysis of this light that Augustine pioneers in the twelfth book of *De Genesi ad Litteram* and the seventh of the *Confessions* find no counterpart in colonial-Quaker discussions, which eschewed Puritan complexities along with Puritan learning.

The culmination of the Augustinian perception of inner light comes rather when Jonathan Edwards turns his powers of definition upon it, in his 1734 sermon *A Divine and Supernatural Light, Immediately Imparted to the Soul by the Spirit of God:*

This spiritual and divine light does not consist in any impression made upon the imagination. It is no . . . idea of an outward light or glory, or any beauty or form or countenance, or a visible lustre or brightness of any object . . . .

[It] is not the suggesting of any new truths or propositions not contained in the word of God. This . . . is inspiration; such as the prophets and apostles had, and such as some enthusiasts pretend to . . . .

It is not every affecting view that men have of the things of religion . . . . A person . . . may be liable to be affected with the story of Jesus Christ . . . . Yea, he may be affected with it without believing it; as well as a man may be affected with what he reads in a romance, or sees acted in a stage-play . . . .

But I proceed to show . . . Positively what this spiritual and divine light is.

And it may be thus described: A true sense of the divine excellency of the things revealed in the word of God, and a conviction of the truth and reality of them thence arising . . . . There is a divine and superlative glory in these things . . . . He that is spiritually enlightened truly apprehends and sees it, or has a sense of it . . . .

It is not a thing that belongs to reason, to see the beauty and loveliness of spiritual things; it is not a speculative thing, but depends on the sense of the heart. Reason indeed is necessary in order to it, as it is by reason only that we are become the subjects of the means of it . . . . But if we take reason strictly, not for the faculty of mental perception in general, but for . . . a power of inferring by arguments . . ., the perceiving of spiritual beauty and excellency no more belongs to reason, than it belongs to the sense of feeling to perceive colours, or to the power of seeing to perceive the sweetness of food . . . . Reason's work is to perceive truth and not excellency . . . . Reason may determine that a countenance is beautiful to others, it may determine that honey is sweet to others; but it will never give me a perception of its sweetness.[76]

Edwards's contemporary, John Woolman, a compassionate Quaker tailor and abolitionist of West New Jersey, enjoins his readers to remember "that in this World we are but Sojourners."[77] His *Journal* of "this journey" of his own life recounts how, as a boy, he went from school one afternoon, sat down out of sight of his playmates, and read the 22nd chapter of *Revelations*: "He shewed me a pure River of Water of Life, clear as Chrystal, proceeding out of the Throne of God and of the Lamb," which drew his mind, he says, to seek after that pure habitation. It was the *sweetness* of the occasion that he said remained fresh in his memory.

He went through the usual Puritan experiences of a severe illness followed by inner struggles, failures and successes, until at length,

that Word which is as a Fire and a Hammer, broke and dissolved my rebellious Heart, and then my Cries were put up in Contrition; and in the multitude of his Mercies I found inward Relief . . . . I was often sad . . . . and . . . sought Desarts and lonely Places, and there, with Tears, did confess my Sins to God . . . . While I silently ponder on that Change wrought in me, I find no

Language equal to it . . . . This white Stone and new Name is known rightly by such only as have it.[78]

Perhaps the penultimate Augustinian utterance of the colonial period comes from the Quaker preacher William Leddra, who on the eve of his hanging 14 March 1661 on Boston Common, wrote his Quaker acquaintances from prison:

The sweet influences of the Morning-Star, like a Flood distilling into my innocent Habitation, hath so filled me with the joy of the Lord in the Beauty of Holiness, that my Spirit is as if it did not Inhabit a Tabernacle of Clay, but is wholly swallowed up in the Bosom of Eternity, from whence it had its Being.[79]

Chapter 3

The Sectarian and Migratory Extension of the Pilgrimage

I'm just a poor wayfaring stranger
A-travelling through this world of woe . . . .
I'm just a-going over Jordan,
I'm just a-going over home.

—18TH-CENTURY WHITE SPIRITUAL

WILLIAM PENN spoke in the language of the pilgrimage, as when he said: *"through many Tribulations are we to enter the Rest and City of God."*[80] Penn opened the door of Pennsylvania to his fellow sojourners of whatever nationality and soon presided over a motley invasion: Scotch-Irish—who of course brought the pilgrimage with their uncompromising brand of Presbyterianism, English Quakers and, among others, a variety of German sects, Baptist and Pietist. Only a sprinkling of the Germans in Pennsylvania in the colonial period were Lutheran, but they too hewed to the pilgrimage; Luther himself, after all, had been an Augustinian monk. The Baptist Germans turned out to be near relatives religiously, as well as close political allies of the Quakers.

Anabaptism arose on the Continent strikingly like Puritanism in England, with the same academic grounding and the

37

same vision of a purified churh. The outstanding German Anabaptist, Balthasar Hubmaier, doctor of theology and professor of philosophy at the University of Ingolstadt, wrote a tract in 1526, *Twelve Articles of Christian Belief*, that could almost have been written two generations later by a Cambridge University Puritan. It holds, for instance, that baptism and the Lord's Supper, as the only valid sacraments, bind believers to Christ in the mystical union that brings salvation.

Not only did Anabaptism and Puritanism tend to converge; they had a long history of subsurface interaction. The first congregation of Calvinistic, or Particular Baptists sprang from what appears to have been the original Independent church, that of Henry Jacob in London. (*Independent* refers to the Congregationalists who claimed not to have separated from the Church of England—which is what the bulk of American Puritans were.) The first English Pietist, or General Baptist church sprang from John Smyth's congregation in Holland, which had had an intimate association with our Plymouth Pilgrims before either left England. Many English groups felt a powerful attraction in Holland to the Mennonite position. The Mennonites there, appropriately called *Waterlanders*, represented the mildest of the three main branches of Mennonites, who so named themselves after the death of their leader, Menno Simons, a West Friesland priest who had been converted to conservative Anabaptism about 1536. Germantown, Pennsylvania became the first of many settlements founded by Mennonites in America.

Baptism had the meaning to the Baptists (who were congregationalists) that the covenant had to the Congregationalist Puritans. The *covenant* was a short-paragraph contract or pledge of commitment to Christ which the adult joining the church repeated in the manner of an oath before the congregation. The Congregationalist regarded it as his formal acceptance of proferred Grace, and felt bound by it to God and the congregation, simultaneously assuming part of the church obligation of stewardship over the community as a whole. *Baptist* is short for *Anabaptist*, which means a believer in re-baptism. The early Anabaptists had already been baptized in infancy in the Roman Catholic, Lutheran, or Anglican Church, and they insisted on repetition of the ceremony because they believed only in individually-responsible commitment to Christ and the church. The controversy over the validity of baptism before adulthood is one of the oldest dividers in Christian annals. The controversy over the *manner* of baptism—immersion or sprinkling—did not loom as large. Baptists themselves came to no agreement on that for a long time, and some eminent Puritan Congregationalists, like Jacob and the first Charles Chauncy in New England, believed in "dipping."

The burning questions about baptism, however, did nothing to divide Baptists from Puritans in their common pilgrim orientation. Bunyan was a Baptist (he happened to be an immersionist), and he spoke for every pilgrim society, regardless of denomination. Increase Mather, who licensed the first American reprint of *The Pilgrim's Progress*, participated in the forming of a Baptist church in Boston around 1680—quite a reversal of the Baptist-persecuting days of not many years before. Roger Williams, sometime minister of the Pilgrims and of the Salem Puritans, turned Baptist (non-immersionist) for three or four months in Providence.

The early Baptists also had much in common with early Quakers. George Fox, after all, began as a Baptist and recruited most of his Quaker followers from Baptist groups. Ann Hutchinson's sister Katherine, who according to Winthrop "infected" Williams with Anabaptistry, herself turned Quaker in time. The Dissenters who came from England and *continued* to dissent, tended to become either Baptist, Quaker, or Antinomian—or all three at different times. Most of the people the Court at Newtown banished as Antinomians, who later became Baptist or Quaker, had been bona fide members of Congregational churches in Massachusetts. Every heretical position that English Puritanism contained within itself in precarious balance, the Baptist position retained with identical propensities, as we can see starkly from a roster of Baptist ministers in London in 1731, which shows seven Antinomian, seven Calvinist, six Arminian, three Unitarian, and two Seventh-Day. The very heat of the disputes between Baptists and Quakers in Rhode Island and Providence Plantations may betray more family kinship than unrelatedness.

The distinguished Presbyterian historians Robert Baillie, Thomas Edwards, and Ephraim Pagitt in the middle of the 17th century charged that both Separatist and non-separating Congregationalism had derived from Anabaptism—which is what Elizabeth's archbishop Whitgift had said about Cartwright Presbyterianism. The English Congregationalists, as the Presbyterians before them, indignantly rejected this interpretation. But the Rhineland emerges more and more with recent scholarship as a crucible for Puritanism, Anabaptism, and Pietism, all three. The soil had been well conditioned there for religious revivals and doctrinal creativity by three centuries of endemic mysticism. This was Dominican mysticism, which got transplanted to that vicinity with the extraordinary concentration of Dominican nunneries in the Rhineland beginning in the late 13th century.

Coming down to the 16th century, Leonard Trinterud finds that principally in the Rhineland centers of Zürich, Basel, and Strassburg occurred a cultivation of Augustinian piety before Calvin's work and distinct from Luther's, and that more ministers and theological students found their way from England to the Rhineland in the Marian exile than to Calvin's Geneva.[81]

Perhaps the fullest-flooding pipeline of extremer Puritan and sectarian attitudes to England can be found emanating in the late 16th and early 17th century from the vicinity of the Rhine's mouth in cities like Antwerp, Amsterdam, Rotterdam, Flushing, Middelburg, and Delft, where English entrepreneurs maintained chapels and chaplains, where English garrisons (in the case of Dutch centers of resistance to Spain) did the same; where English exiles established their own churches; and where universities, like those of Leyden and Franeker, employed Dissenting clergymen in their faculties. The leading systematic theologians, Cartwright and Ames, were among the numerous English Puritans who, at one time or another, exerted far-reaching authority while residing in this region.[82]

Augustine, however, had been introduced into England long before the Reformation, no doubt by that other Augustine, the missionary to turn-of-the-6th-century Britain. Alfred the Great actually translated the first Augustine's *Soliloquies* into Old English. Puritanism became indigenous in medieval England and emerged in Tudor times in the thought and works of the great Bible translator William Tyndale and his associates in and before 1534. Tyndale, who had been with Luther at Wittenberg in 1524, was already by 1534 adapting Rhineland religious theories to a native English tradition of Augustinian piety as represented by Wyclif, among others.[83]

But, granting this, the influence of Calvin remains hardly beyond dispute as fundamental in English Calvinism. Thomas

Cartwright definitively formulated English Presbyterianism and, though he reflected the native tradition of Wyclif and Tyndale, learned Calvin's system at first hand in Geneva, the better to transplant it.[84] Calvinism, we have noted, represents another strain of Augustinian piety anyway.

Calvin was French and became identified with Geneva, near Zwingli's Zürich. A parishioner of Zwingli's, Conrad Grebel, organized Anabaptism as a separate denomination; and Zwingli was a pioneer of the refined covenant theology identified with English Congregationalists which Tyndale apparently introduced into England from Rhineland currency; English exiles in Wittenberg published a covenant-based confession of faith as early as 1554. So the interrelations weave. Another of the most influential thinkers on English Puritans, also on Calvin, was Oecolampadius of Basel, and another, the French political philosopher Jan Bodin. Perry Miller has ingeniously traced the dialectic of such important Puritan formulators as Perkins, Richardson, and Ames to the passionately-Platonic Calvinist at the University of Paris, Peter Ramus; subsequent scholarship indicates that Ramus also instigated much of the theory of church polity that led to Congregationalism.[85] George Sabine has shown the influence on England of the anonymous *Vindiciae contra tyrannos*, first published in Paris in 1579 and since attributed to Hubert Lanquet, Philippe du Plessis-Mornay, or some other Frenchman.[86]

But we need hardly belabor the extent of English Puritan indebtedness to the Continent, especially the Rhineland, Geneva, and France. The Reformation decisively began in Saxony.

* * *

A DUNKER (i.e. immersionist Baptist) Johann Conrad Beissel, who had been a baker in Eberbach, Germany, founded the curious cloister at Ephrata, Pennsylvania, on Cocalico Creek, in 1732. It was a celibate community for both sexes that employed itself, while it lasted, in medieval arts and crafts. Beissel is most notable for the hymns he composed to be sung at sunrise and sunset in connection with vigils and fasts. Professedly attempting to imitate the aeolian harp, his choir sang in falsetto with, according to tradition, an ethereal effect, well suited to the quiet mystic ecstasy aimed for.

The first of Beissel's hymnbooks published at Ephrata (1747) bore the title (in translation) *The Call of the Solitary and Deserted Turtle Dove*, its inspiration the peace-conducive verse from the *Song of Songs*: "The time of the singing of birds is come, and the voice of the turtle is heard in our land." This was a favorite book and passage of the Puritans too, fondly quoted, for instance, by Cotton Mather in 1721.[87] One of Beissel's later hymnbooks had the pilgrim title *Zionitischer Rosengarten*; and his most ambitious "motet," *Gott ein Herrscher aller Heiden*, for seven voices, concerns God's leading the faithful toward Zion: *"wenn er Zion schön wird schmücken,"* etc.[88]

The war-ravaged Palatinate sects who migrated to Pennsylvania in large numbers usually felt music to be as much an aid to their piety and inner-light mysticism as the Quakers and (to a somewhat less degree) the Puritans felt it an interference. The Quakers did not follow Augustine in conceiving the inner voice as musical. But the *object* of encouraging or banning music was the same—the facilitating of the pilgrimage.

Perhaps the most remarkable of the Pietist groups in Pennsylvania was a chapter of forty "true Rosicrucians" who landed at Philadelphia in 1694 clad as medieval monks. Under the leadership of an intense young mystic from German Transylvania, Johannes Kelpius, they established a monastery on the "Ridge" overlooking the Wissahickon and called themselves "The Contented of the God-loving Soul." Kelpius was a follower of the father of German Pietism, the kindly Philipp Spener, and was also steeped in the earlier mysticism of Jacob Böhme—as evidently was that strange Puritan, Samuell Gorton, founder of Warwick, Rhode Island.

Kelpius habitually went to a cave for solitary contemplation despite the fact that he was dying of tuberculosis; he deliberately courted a wintry death. While he lived, the monks sang rhapsodic hymns, mostly written by Kelpius, in their log tabernacle. The best of the hymns is probably the one entitled *Colloquium of the Soul with its Self over her Long Living Purification. Set in a Pensive Longing in the Wilderness* (1698).

> O Blessedest Dying!
> Which break'st death no less! . . . .
> Oh, break once the junctures of this turning wheel!
> And shorten the Path which so tedious is still!
> And make the way straiter unto Sion Hill! . . . .

> *O Take me from Me!*
> *That I allways may hover*
> *One spirit with thee!*[89]

This is a sample of its interminable Augustinian-ecstatic content. The Tabernacle, which the monks abandoned at Kelpius's death, was taken over in the 1730s and rebuilt by a group of self-styled pilgrims calling themselves the Zionitic brotherhood.

The last and most important body of German Pietists to arrive in America was that descended from John Hus, under their new name, the *Unitas Fratrum*, or Moravian Brethren. A small colony of them entered Pennsylvania in 1740 and established their first permanent settlement on the Lehigh River in 1742. This they named Bethlehem from one of their favorite Christmas hymns. Bethlehem thereafter occupied the center of the Moravian colonizing-missionizing network that came to include the towns Nazareth, Lititz, Lancaster, Salem, and then others. Their patron and second founder, Count Nikolaus Ludwig von Zinzendorf, a passionate mystic and prolific hymn-writer, personally helped establish the new Bethlehem. He had previously opened his estate at Berthelsdorf, Saxony to members of the faith, naming his refugee settlement *Herrnhut* (Home of God), and he directed and largely financed the movement to his death in 1760.

At Bethlehem the Moravians founded what they called the "Church of the Pilgrims." Their assiduous cultivation of music, instrumental and choral, included the custom of trombone choirs from about 1735 on, to announce the death of a church member. The tune they most commonly used, apparently, was the Hans Leo Hassler passion chorale known in English as *O Sacred Head*, which that Lutheran pilgrim Johann Sebastian Bach harmonized variously and exquisitely in several large works. The German words used in the funeral ceremony in Moravian villages, as translated by the Moravians into English in the 19th century, went in part:

> *A pilgrim, us preceding*
> *Departs unto his home . . .*
> *O joy! the chain to sever*
> *Which burdens pilgrims here,*
> *To dwell with Christ forever . . . .*[80]

The pervasion of the pilgrimage in Pennsylvania had implications of a subtle and easily-missed kind. They proved the more important in that Pennsylvania provided one of the great reservoirs for future settlement of the country west and south. Daniel Boone was a Pennsylvania Quaker with Baptist leanings who combined the serenity and the restlessness of a pilgrim and surprisingly talked about the pretty flowers and fruits and the happiness he felt in the perilous "howling wilderness" of Kentucky in 1770. For our inquiry it hardly matters whether his amanuensis, John Filson, did most of the composing of Boone's narrative, since Filson also represents the western Pennsylvanian going south at the same time and carrying with him either Quaker or Presbyterian piety. The Moravians had already penetrated systematically into North Carolina, where Boone went before proceeding to Kentucky.

Unreconstructed Puritans streamed steadily into the middle and southern colonies both from New and Old England. They early formed a large proportion of the population of Maryland, large enough to neutralize the famous toleration act barely passed over their opposition by the Catholic majority on the Council. Part of the Puritan congregation of Dorchester, Massachusetts migrated directly to South Carolina and founded the Dorchester there.[91] Quakers, including the preacher-hero Wenlock Christisen, whom Endecott had angrily sentenced to death in Boston, settled in prosperous plantations in Maryland, as elsewhere along the seaboard and in the West Indies.[92] Scottish immigrants from Ulster began to settle along the Eno and the Haw in western North Carolina about 1738, having pressed south from Pennsylvania with Germans, English, and Welsh; they sent their ministerial candidates to Princeton.[93] These are merely random examples of a considerable southerly and westerly movement of pilgrim-oriented pioneers.

A discerning observer said a couple of years before 1700 that there were then few or no Dissenters in Virginia—not enough to set up a meeting-house, except for three or four meetings of Quakers and one of Presbyterians.[94] But Thomas Jefferson says that by the outbreak of the Revolution Dissenters had come to comprise *two-thirds* of Virginia's population.[95] The Valley of Virginia, in particular, had become a stronghold of Baptist, Presbyterian, and Pietist settlers, though unfranchised.

As the Quakers of Philadelphia influenced Jefferson during

his several sojourns in Pennsylvania, so the Dissenters in Virginia significantly influenced such non-Dissenters as Patrick Henry and James Madison. Henry imbibed this influence not only from neighboring Dissenters beyond the social pale, but at home from his mother. Henry's father was a Scotch Anglican and his mother an English Presbyterian. She, furthermore, proved susceptible to New Light Presbyterianism and frequently took young Henry to hear the revivalist Samuel Davies after Davies settled in Hanover County in 1747. Many later southerners of eminence, including James Knox Polk, Stonewall Jackson, and Woodrow Wilson, were Puritan types.

While the pilgrimage as an era was closing in New England, the New England version of the pilgrimage took a new lease on life in the back country, north and south. After the hymns and fuguing-tunes of the stentorian Boston choirmaster William Billings had gone out of style in the old Puritan centers of New England, they had a lustier vogue than ever on the frontiers to the south, where the sectarians sang, for instance, Isaac Watt's *Jordan* as set by Billings:

There is a land of pure delight where saints immortal reign . . .
Sweet fields beyond the swelling flood stand dress'd in living
*   green*
So to the Jews old Canaan stood while Jordan roll'd between.[96]

The New England clergyman Peter Williams translated part of a Welsh hymn in the middle or late 18th century that also flowed south with the tide of migration: "Guide me, O thou great Jehovah, Pilgrim through this barren land . . . ." Where Boone had camped in Kentucky remote from white settlers in 1770, such pilgrim songs echoed resoundingly in the camp-meetings of a few decades later; presently the Methodists reinforced the Baptists, Pietists, and Presbyterians with the same Zionism. The Methodists and Baptists imparted it to Negroes, who espoused it with comparable emotion.[97] All of these groups expressed their deep sentiments in such well-known hymns as "Shall we gather at the river?," "I'm bound for the land of Canaan," "I heard of a City called Heaven," "I'm a pilgrim," "I'm just a poor wayfaring stranger," "One more river to cross," "Deep River," and "Will the waters be chilly?" Also:

> *I looked over Jordan and what did I see? . . .*
> *A band of angels comin' after me,*
> *Comin' for to carry me home.*

"I'll labor night and day to be a pilgrim," said John Bunyan in one of his hymns that these groups adopted. In the 18th century another Englishman, Robert Seagrave, wrote a hymn with the injunction "Cease, ye pilgrims, cease to mourn," and Charles Wesley wrote one with the call, "Come, let us anew our journey pursue." These hymns are still widely sung, as are many written in the 19th century on the same themes. A number of 19th-century hymns allude to the "homeward way" or "homeward road"; "I can never, never lose my way," one goes, and another: "in that light of life I'll walk, till traveling days are done." A lady hymnwriter, Fanny Crosby, says in one of her hymns:

> *All along my pilgrim journey,*
> *Saviour, let me walk with Thee.*

A fitting conclusion to this verse is one from a different hymn of hers:

> *Till I reach the golden strand*
> *Just beyond the river.*

"Singing to welcome the pilgrims of the night," the refrain of still another hardy 19th-century hymn ends. "On Jordan's stormy banks," "Gently lead me by the hand, Pilgrims in a desert land," and "Swift shall pass thy pilgrim days" are other strains that followed the sun across the continent.

The folk-sense of a pilgrimage must have been very strong, to judge from the number of times the pioneers founded Zion all over again. They founded a Zion, Maryland, Arkansas, Illinois, Missouri, New Jersey, and South Carolina; a Zionville, North Carolina; a Zionsville, Indiana; a Zion Hill, Mississippi; and a Mount Zion, Georgia, Illinois, Iowa, North Carolina, and West Virginia; a New Canaan, Connecticut; a New Galilee, Pennsylvania; a Jerusalem, Rhode Island and Ohio; a Mt. Judea, Arkansas; a Jordan, South Carolina; and a Pilgrim, Kentucky.

The Mormons, whose original leaders came out of New England where their ancestors had had roots going back to the middle-17th century in Massachusetts, proceeded from Vermont to upstate New York and eventually on a westward pilgrimage of endless hundreds of miles, regarding themselves (like the Pilgrims crossing the Atlantic in the *Mayflower*) as the saints bound to reestablish the true church. They named the large stream that flowed just west of their Salt Lake settlement the River Jordan, and the great canyon in the south, Zion. Out of the midst of Zion Canyon rises a majestic rocky eminence, and this they called the Great White Throne.

Chapter 4

The Psychology (or Psychosis?) of Bereavement

*. . . It is not the teares of the eye, but the blood of the
heart that your sinnes must cost . . . .*
—THOMAS HOOKER, *The Sovles Preparation
for Christ,* 1632

My Friends, your Griefs *can't be* Cured. *But cannot you
then be* Cured *by your* Griefs?
COTTON MATHER, *Insanabilia,* 1714

*Is it derangement to be always awake, always sure, never
obscure and dreaming?*
—SOREN KIERKEGAARD, *Repetition,* 1843

THE PILGRIM trudged uphill under the weight of a heavy
burden. He longed for relief, rest, peace; for a higher unity
and harmony or, as he conceived it, a going home. "To wish
for Death is to wish for Life," Hugh Peter, Williams's successor
in the pulpit at Salem and Cromwell's "Puritan Archbishop,"
repeated a Christian commonplace from the Tower of London
when he faced his imminent execution in utmost anguish. He
did not need the Tower to induce an abnormal mental state;

he had been subject to psychotic depression periodically all his life. The great, somberly-brooding Cromwell, incidentally, had been subject to habitual melancholy and even to delusions. (Bunyan's pilgrim was weary of an "inward sickness.") A couple of Peter's friends spoke of the unhappy end of that preacher's "wearisome pilgrimage."[98]

Peter could not bring himself to welcome his "translation" the way Leddra had on the eve of *his* execution. Within a page of saying that to wish for death is to wish for life, Peter had said: "I say, Life is sweet, and Death terrible."[99] Which begins to suggest that when Puritans expressed a death wish coupled with contempt for this world, they may actually have been wishing for the correction of something amiss here below. The statement, "To wish for Death is to wish for Life," on the face of it implies that life has little to offer, that death in fact has more life to offer than life itself. Christian theology of course puts a different face upon it, but the theology, we must remember, also grew out of profound despair.

Whatever the cause of the despair, this emotion or one related to it, frequently asserts itself in Puritan literature. In the passionate poetic language of Augustine, Edwards said:

I had vehement longings of soul after God and Christ, and after more holiness, wherewith my heart seemed to be full, and ready to break; which often brought to my mind the words of the Psalmist, Psal. cxix. 28. *My soul breaketh for the longing it hath.*[100]

This is the language of bereavement. The whole idea of devaluing the world and longing brokenheartedly to quit it, even if what one actually grieved was the inevitability of quitting it, suggests bereavement. And when the Puritan tried to abandon the world yet at the same time transform it, his stoic exaltation had about it a character that in other contexts has been associated with grief-maddened hysteria. Puritans like Hooker went through a period that gave every appearance of temporary insanity in the process of their conversion, and this was a surprisingly universal experience among Puritans up through the upheaval of the English civil war. Hooker said he could compare with any man for fears,[101] and in one of his autobiographically-based treatises said "It is possible for the most stubborne sinners upon earth to get a broken heart . . . ."[102] "A *contrite*, and broken heart is an *House* wherein *God* dwells," said Williams.[103] Psalm 51, which says the sacrifice acceptable to God is a broken spirit, a broken and contrite heart, struck almost too responsive a chord in Puritans.

They, of course, always bereaved their past sins: the burden they bore on their backs was a burden of guilt. "Our *Sin* is the Cause of our *Grief*," said Cotton Mather. "Our *sin* has made us worthy of *Grievous Things*."[104] But, in reality, it is the grievous things that have caused the grief—as Mather clearly sees; for he goes on to say that our sin *ought* now to be our grief.[105] Even if it were their own deaths the Puritans were bereaving in advance, it is likely that the *"Grievous Things"* that had come to pass turned their attention that way.

When Hooker said that adversity had killed its thousands but prosperity would kill its ten thousands,[106] he obliquely betrayed that the pilgrimage probably depended on a hard life. As a general sense of wellbeing crept over New England, the pious Puritans scarcely could keep up their grave concentration on death; and their pious children could scarcely manage to bring off convulsive conversion experiences. Just going to church began to be drudgery. From about the time Hooker saw ominous signs of prosperity on the horizon, the magistrates took official note of the appearance of gay apparel and other alarming evidences of worldly vanity; and the clergy this early got into the habit of deploring the "declension" of the people, while trying to revive Puritanism as it was thought to have been in 1630. Increase Mather's brother Eleazar, the first pastor at Northampton, warned his congregation in 1671 just before he died that

> Outward prosperity is a worm at the root of godliness, so that Religion dies when the World thrives, *Deut.* 28.47. & 32.15 . . . . Oh consider, the time was when [there was] less of the world, but was there not more of Heaven? less Trading, Buying, Selling, but more Praying, more watching over our own hearts, more close walking; less plenty, and less iniquity . . . . There is sad declinings in the Spirit of the Churches . . . . The dayes wherein you live are backsliding times, *evil dayes, 2 Tim.* 3.1. times of great degeneracy and Apostacy . . . .[107]

The pilgrimage remained a powerful binding ingredient in New England culture, but its weakening is detectable almost from the moment the first Puritan foot touched shore in the new Israel.

Moving to a new home had been sad in the first place. Then

the severe privations and uncertainties of the initial winters and summers, when an appalling proportion of the planters died and the remainder staggered grimly through lingering illness, but a perpetual pall on life. But in a few years, with familiarity of the countryside, with the first overwhelming odds gradually reduced and health returned, the wilderness looked rather challenging than paralyzing, and charming than "hideous." Bradford discloses that it took more than four and a half years for the Pilgrims to begin to perceive the pleasantness of their new country, but that then everybody did.[108] In less than seven more years he was complaining of the neglect of the church in the scramble for bigger farms and a higher standard of living.[109]

When sadness went up in work, it was apparent that a hard life by itself did not fully account for otherworldly bereavement. It was hardness *plus* the intimidated or frustrated sense of not being able to do anything about the bleak situation with any amount of good intentions, rigorous thought, or hard work. When these human agencies finally brought measurable results, the zest of work, even though overhard, lifted the pilgrims' weight of despondency. Every new thrust farther into the wilderness, however, revived afresh the pilgrim feelings of those who had wrested the first beachhead. All over again came the sadness of moving, the privations, uncertainties and disease, and the paralyzing prospect of everything to be done against overwhelming odds while still half homesick.

The Puritans did not require the wilderness to feel bereaved; they already felt that way before they left England. It was in the wilderness that they worked themselves out of this mood in time. The "American pilgrimage" can be viewed in a large sense as the steady journey *away* from the other world back toward this one. Although the early generations clung to the reverse conception of their journey, at first with jealous intensity and eventually with loyal lip-service, and through the ever-renewed frontier sustained the original sense of bereavement in some strength, we must seek its wellsprings abroad.

Puritanism was a long-frustrated movement in England, and it came into being as a by-product of the protracted, tearing travail of the birth of modern times. It is now a truism that Protestantism itself arose along with the national state and capitalism. It is an even older truism that English Puritanism arose with the "new learning" and also with the enclosure movement (the fencing of farms into sheep pastures); and the enclosure movement hastened the early industrial revolution, mass unemployment, and overall English potency. Rapid change; too much war; sharp dislocations of traditional patterns, brought stress and strain and pain with their usual stimulation of mystic religion and of anguished cries for reform. "In pain of love towards beauty," Plotinus had said that persons escape to their spiritual home. It is hard to avoid the conclusion that such a pervasive mood of bereavement as Augustinian-ecstatic Puritanism represented on an international scale, came at least partly from a trauma of the times —or a mis-diagnosis of the times—and not merely from individual personal grief.

Shepard and Bradford may never have recovered emotionally from having been orphaned; Winthrop and Browne may never have recovered emotionally from desultory illness (Augustine, Calvin, Cartwright, and Ames were chronically ill); but everybody who had been orphaned or had had a long illness did not turn mystic Puritan; many Puritans (like John Cotton) who were not orphans and were hardly ever ill, did; Jonathan Edwards is a good example of a Puritan who felt grief-stricken before he had ever known personal bereavement. The more of the evidence we review, the more it suggests that some general dislocation in the environment rather than —or in addition to—personal misfortune, self-pity, or sad temperament started these Dissenters trudging forth on their grief-wracked, solitary, renunciatory, romantic pilgrimage.

Robert Browne, who dramatically pioneered the Separatist position of the Pilgrims (and at length returned to the fold of the state church as essentially a Presbyterian), represents much more the norm than the extreme he has been taken to be, in his path to Puritanism. He, by the way, considered the germinating medium of Puritanism to have been "schooles," "the Vniversitie of Cambridge," and private tutoring "in families & houshouldes, as is the manner of that countrie." After Cambridge he himself turned schoolteacher for three years and, measuring the out-of-joint world by his informed religious idealism, found all his conscientiousness unavailing. The world, he says, "being so corrupt as it is, & the times so perilous," he "greatly misliked the vvantes & defaultes, vvwhich he savve euerie vvhere . . . ." If Puritanism were economic, Puritans did not see it or understand it as an economic problem. Instead, as Browne says of himself,

he fell into great care, & vvas soare greeued vvhile he long considered manie thinges amisse, & the case of all, to be the vvofull
and lamentable state off the church.[110]

This can stand as the typical process of deepening Puritanism:
a grieving from the wrong-doing of the times, which led to an
all-out turning to the church and then to a determination to
correct it in order that it might correct the world.

Winthrop brooded on the cheapening of life in England in
1629:

> This lande growes wearye of her Inhabitantes, so as man
> which is the most pretious of all Creatures, is heere more vile and
> base, then the earthe they treade vpon: as children neighbours
> and friendes (especially if they be poore) are rated the greatest
> burdens, which if things were right, would be the chiefest earthly
> blessings.[111]

But "things" were not right, and this became immediately a
religious problem to Winthrop, as it had become to Browne.
He did not want an economic but a religious (and political)
revolution—or counter-revolution. Instead of talking of imminent economic ruin as such, the Puritans talked of the
coming wrath of God. "All other Churches of Europe are
brought to desolation, and it cannot be, but the like Judgment
is cominge vpon vs," Winthrop concludes.[112] He had already
spoken of the "evill & declining tymes" when this prophetic
spirit first fully seized him. "My dear wife, I am verily per-
suaded, God will bringe some heavye Affliction upon this lande,
& that speedylye . . . ."[113]

When Robert Cushman visited Plymouth in 1621, intending
to return soon for good, he preached a memorable sermon
which he published the year following in London. In the
Epistle dedicatory he expresses a widely-held conviction that
the American wilderness offered refuge to the saintly saving
remnant who managed to escape the Turkish slavery or Popish
tyranny by which God might be about to punish His people.[114]
The renowned Hooker capped the climax of this thinking in
his sensational farewell sermon of 1633, on the doctrine *"That
God may justly leave off a people, and unchurch a Nation"*:

. . . Miseries are nigh by all probabilities . . . . All things are ripe
for ruine . . . . God may leave a Nation that is but in outward

covenant with him [as the Jews], and why not England? . . . . We play mock-holy-day with God, the Gospell we make it our pack-horse: God is going, his glory is departing, England hath seene her best dayes, and now evill dayes are befalling us: God is packing up his Gospell, because no body will buy his wares, nor come to his price. Oh lay hands on God! and let him not goe out of your coasts, he is going, stop him . . . . And marke what I say, the poore native Turks and Infidels shall have a cooler summer parlour in hell then you . . . .[115]

Hooker, at any rate, was departing; he had divined a negative prognosis on the ailment of his native country. Four years later, in Ann Hutchinson's trial, it came out that when she had drawn within sight of Boston and looked on the "meanness of the place," she said that "if she had not a sure word that England should be destroyed her heart would shake."[116] Her hearers did not like her appeal to Hooker's authority; his disciple John Eliot went so far as to deny that Hooker would have held such a view. Her hearers also did not like her dire prophecies on the downfall of the Bay. But in the next generation the Mathers took up Hooker's sentiments toward England and started applying them to New England. "The Lord is farre gone, when there is no enquiry whether he be gone or no," said Eleazar at Northampton in 1671.[117] "Oh that I might prove a false Prophet when I often say, *The Gospel I fear is going, the Lord Jesus is departing from these Coasts,'*" Increase wrote in Boston in 1672.[118] And this was barely the beginning of Increase's long exploitation of this theme.

Puritanism obviously meant in part a reaction of pain to external conditions, and a determination to reform the existing order. Whenever Christianity has been on the upsurge, it has bent itself to transforming the "evil world." Was Puritanism a healthy reaction to a sick world, a sick reaction to a sick world, or a sick reaction to a misjudged situation—if indeed at bottom a reaction to external stimuli at all?

The mood of Puritanism seems almost identical to that of Plato and Augustine, its double fountainhead. Both Plato and Augustine lived in a world they thought they saw collapsing about them. Plato watched the humiliating defeat of Athens and the failure of Athenian democracy during the all-corrosive, unhinging Peloponnesian War; the sentencing of his teacher and Athen's greatest citizen to death; and even, though Plato did not quite realize it, the doom of the city-state as a political unit. Plato's philosophy is essentially a religion, conceived in grief and despair. By its very attempt to transcend grief and despair, it deepened the melancholy that had already overcast Greek thought for centuries in its realization of the limits of a life span.

This melancholy had become a cloying malaise by Augustine's time. Besides enduring excruciating personal guilts and the dashing of his dearest hopes with the death of his son at the brink of manhood, Augustine saw everywhere the signs of advanced decay in Roman culture. The sack of the city of Rome itself in 410 moved him to write his *City of God* to absolve Christianity. Plato and Augustine must have felt much like Hooker when Hooker predicted the destruction of England and said "England hath seene her best dayes, and now evill dayes are befalling us." England *appeared* to Hooker as Rome must have appeared to Augustine, or Athens to Plato. They all three also had in common a refusal to succumb to their times. They strove to salvage the values of the passing order with a higher idealism, or utopianism, than ever, and to build a world *within* more worthy and enduring amidst the ruins without, one not subject to change or to corruption by moth or rust.

IF PURITANISM were psychosis, it would have to be other than the usual tests. Like Plato and Augustine, Puritans were more, rather than less, responsible—toward themselves and society— and more self-reliant, self-controlled, and astutely discriminating in matters of law, morality, and duty. If spoken to, they answered; and their answer was more, rather than less logical, coherent, and restrained than the norm.

One school of thought, however, regards Puritanism as a carefully cultivated illusion.

> *Art fancy sick, or turned a sot,*
> *To catch at shadows which are not?*

as Flesh says to Spirit in Ann Bradstreet's poem. Another school (that of the Puritans themselves, including Ann Bradstreet) regards Puritanism as wide-eyed realism. Either was, this kind of illusion or realism has been held by so many, often the best, in the last 23 centuries than an ingrained psychosis, if this makes psychosis, woud have to be considered nearly normal. Either way, or both ways at once, the Puritan met his conception of reality with an unflinching steadiness and courage that brought him through his pilgrimage in admirable control of his psychosis, or that neutralized it, if he had it. Men like Shepard, Edwards, and Cotton Mather did not crack up. When they died, it was with minds at peace.

But a sense of horror, of futility, and of doubt never strayed far from the Puritan mentality. No wonder the word "grave" or "gravity" recurs with such piston-like insistence in the contemporary descriptions of leading Puritans, or that austerity should run as one of several deep currents in the Puritan complex. Part of this, of course, may have risen from nothing more than mature reflectiveness. But the Puritans coupled maturity of reflection with a childish credulity. The redoubtable Shepard, for instance, recalls that he and his wife settled some months in a house in Heddon, five miles from Newcastle, which a known witch had just vacated. For four or five nights in a row they were much troubled by noises, which they overcame by prayer.[119] Mrs. Thomas Hooker explained a certain earthquake as the Devil's displeasure that Mrs. Dyer's monstrous birth was being discussed.[120] The Puritans spent much of their time collecting "providences," like mysterious coincidences, earthquakes, monster births, etc., an activity that indicates the medieval immediacy and drama of the divine presence to them. On closer inspection, it also indicates a *non*-medieval anxiety, and this looks suspiciously like a morbid fear of that enveloping change which jeopardized the pilgrim premises.

Increase Mather's magnum opus, *Illustrious Providences*, contains chapters on "things preternatural," including haunted houses, demons and possessed persons, apparitions, etc., as well as more reliable and even scientific reporting of unusual phenomena. If he shows his oneness with his time, his time was shifting to the defensive. The underlying defensive character of his observations emerges in such statements as his conclusion on apparitions: "the witlings of this drolling age know not what they do, when they make themselves sport with subjects of this nature."[121] In *Kometographia* (which he, however, spelled in Greek characters), Increase defiantly insists: "It is indubitable that the true Planets and fixed Stars have a natural influence into such things [as droughts, caterpillars, tempests, floods, epidemics, and earthquakes], though the manner of their operation is by us silly Mortals undeclarable."[122] Roger Williams had the same reaction to the comet of 1680 that Increase published in *Heavens Alarm to the World*. Williams wrote the town clerk of Providence: "Black clouds (some years) have hung over Old and New England heads . . . . All fear that this blazing herald from heaven denounceth from the Most High, wars, pestilence, famine, is it not then our wisdom to make and keep peace with God and man?"[123]

One day in April 1695 that anxiety-ridden luminary Cotton Mather went to dine at the home of Judge Samuel Sewall, who, by the way, was suffering great remose for his tragic aberration in voting to admit spectral evidence in the witch "trials" and to execute the accused. Cotton was just wondering what God's meaning could be in smiting more ministers' houses with lightning, proportionably, than others', when a sudden hail storm broke the glass and sent great stones flying to the middle of the room. Cotton and the Sewalls knelt to pray.[124] In his awe-struck *Wonders of the Invisible World*, Cotton says he has set himself "to countermine the whole PLOT of the Devil, against *New-England*," interpreting the outbreak of witchcraft as an attempt of the Devil to regain his territories which the Puritans had taken from the Indians.[125] His *Diary* for 1692 also shows him amenable to the notion of the witchcraft as a reaction of the evil angels to his own personal campaign to revive Puritanism. The fact that Cotton did not escape the throes of this madness was to cost him an anguish of rationalizing the rest of his life.

In the hysteria of the never-ending wars with French and Indians during the witchcraft period, the decade-long general smallpox depredation, the covert instigation of the perilous Revolution of 1689 at Boston, and the near panic over the vanishing of those charter rights which had secured the holy commonwealth, the assault of the new age a-borning seemed something like an attack by ghosts. The forces of urban, commercial secularism and of Copernican and Newtonian science (for the Puritan universe—as in *Paradise Lost*—remained Ptolematic) blurred the pilgrim ideal. It was all inexorable, invisible, and but darkly understood. In induced violent fantasies in the Puritans, as when Increase injected this jarring note in his *Autobiography*: "I am now waiting and praying for an earthquake which shall issue in the downfall of the Lord's enemies, and the exaltation of his kingdom and interests."[126]

JONATHAN EDWARDS said that the pilgrim must struggle through the wilderness up toward Zion against the tendencies and inclination of his own flesh. Whether there may be an element of psychosis or not in going against nature, it certainly sets up a tension both within the pilgrim and between him and the rest of society. The natural man, the Puritans always said, was naturally evil. Edwards's distinguished protégé, Samuel Hopkins, informs us that Edwards "was a great Enemy to young People's unseasonable Company-keeping and Frolicking" and did not allow his eight daughters to be from home after 9 p.m. Hopkins also recalls Edwards's "solemnity and gravity."[127] Almost every Puritan got described as solemn and grave by those who knew him.

At the same time, Puritans thought of themselves as more, and more subtantially happy.

> *My thoughts do yield me more content*
> *Than can thy hours in pleasure spent*

says Ann Bradstreet. The Puritans thought of the happiness they thought they had as something too important to be gay, let alone frivolous about. Roger Williams was typically Puritan in calling for cheerfulness in his *Experiments of Spiritual Health,* but he struck an even more authentic Puritan note when he later talked of "our *eyes* and *cheeks* thus *wet, unwiped.*"[128] Shepard confessed that the preparation of every sermon had cost him tears, that he had wept through the studying of each one.[129] Increase Mather, though one of the gravest Puritans of the lot, says that Puritans *"ought not to be dejected and desponding, but rather cheerful in their way & work.* Thoughts of the Blessed Hope should make them Joyful in their Serving God . . . ." He tells of two old Puritans who came to an inn and, to the surprise of the innkeeper, were very cheerful. "I thought such men as you are had alwayes been Sad and Malancholly," said the innkeeper. To which the ministers replied, *"Let them be so that must go to Hell when they Dye"*; and this so affected the innkeeper that he became a Puritan. Increase concludes by quoting Psalm 42: "Why art thou cast down O my Soul?"[130]

Yet Increase was always pointing out that this was not the time for cheer. "Everybody knows that it is a time of much Affliction with the Church of God in the World," he said in 1685. "Is this a Time for *Jigs* and Galiards!" The very title of the book he said this in reveals a rather cheerless state of mind: *An Arrow against Profane and Promiscuous Dancing.* He had nothing against dancing itself, of course. Like John Cotton, he thought jumping up and down in religious joy was warranted by Scripture. "But our question is concerning *Gynecandrical Dancing* .... viz. of Men and Women .... together"; and this "cannot be tollerated in such a place as *New-England,* without great sin." The people whose esteem is most to be valued— "such as are grave and solid, and wise"—do not, says Increase, agree with "Light Persons" that *"Pantomical Gestures"* are an accomplishment. Another thing in "this debauched Age: frequent *Osculations* amongst those that are not in any Conjugal Relation .... Christians ought to hate such tendencies to *Nicolaitism* ...." And he wonders what the prophet Isaiah would think if he were alive in these days![131]

In 1695 Increase came forth with another wet blanket entitled *Solemn Advice to Young Men, not to walk in the Wayes of their Heart, and in the Sight of their Eyes; but Remember the Day of Judgment,* the second sermon in the series "shewing that sin unrepented of will be bitterness in the Latter END ...." Young men, "when once they have tasted of that forbidden fruit," i.e. "sinfull sports and pastimes," and got "inchanted and intoxicated with it," do not realize that "Original sin hath depraved the whole man" and that the hearts of men "have neither wit nor wile for a good matter." They also do not seem to realize that the eyes are windows through which many sins creep into the heart. "Wherefore men (and in particular young men) ought to be careful not to walk after the sight of their eyes."[132] "The Customs of the People are Vain" (*Jeremiah* 10.3), Increase quotes on the title-page of his *Testimony against Several Prophane and Superstitious Customs* of October 1686. The customs he rails against include stage-plays, health-drinking, dicing, cards, Christmas-keeping, New-Year's gifts, etc. He calls Boston "this Degenerated Town."[133].

It was not that Increase had grown old and cranky; he was not so old at this time and he had spoken to the same effect as a young man; also, the other Puritan ministers agreed with him, especially concerning Boston. Back in the period of King Philip's War he bewailed the haunting of taverns and *"Inordinate Affection to the world."* This early he was clutching vainly at a passing order; and his sense of impending catastrophe was directly proportional to the extent of change.

The Plenty, which our Peace hath been attended with [said Increase in 1676], hath been abused unto great Sensuality . . . . How common hath it been . . . to *haunt Taverns,* and squander away precious hours, nay dayes in publick houses, which if but half that time had been spent in Meditation, Secret Prayer and Self Examination, it had been happy for them . . . . When as our Fathers were *Patterns of Sobriety,* they would not drink a cup of wine nor strong drink, more then should suffice nature . . . men of latter time could transact no business . . . but it must be over a pint of wine or a pot of beer, yea so as that Drunkenness in the sight of man is become a common Sin . . . And . . . yea as to *Pride in respect of Apparel.* People in this Land have not carryed it, as it becometh those that are in a Wilderness, especially when it is such an humbling time . . . . And none more guilty then the poorer sort of people, who will needs go in their Silks and Bravery as if they were the best in the Land. Though it be also too true that the rich and honourable have many of them greatly offended by strange Apparel, especially here in *Boston.* A proud Fashion no sooner comes into the Country, but the *haughty Daughters of Zion in this* place are taking it up, and thereby the whole land is at last infected. What shall we say when men are seen in the Streets with monstrous and horrid *Perriwigs,* and Women with their *Borders and False Locks* and such like whorish Fashions, whereby the anger of the Lord is kindled against the sinfull Land! And now behold how dreadfully is God fulfilling the third chapter of Isaiah . . . . However, certain it is, that the most terrible changes are coming upon the Earth that ever were known since the world began . . . . The powers of Heaven shall be shaken, the Sun shall be turned into darkness, the Moon into blood, and the Stars of Heaven shall loose their shining, Alas who shall live when God doth these things?[134]

Yet with all his agitation over drunkenness and "these private, dark Ale-houses . . . . as being the very Sinks of Sin," Increase's *Wo to Drunkards* has an unsuspected absence of extremism: "I know that in such a great Town as this, there is need of such Houses, and no sober Minister will speak against the Licensing of them; but I wish there be not more of them then there is any need of."[135] Censoriousness, furthermore, is not the principal emphasis in the thought of any of the Mathers. We have to remember, too, the asceticism naturally called forth in wartime, and that the covenant theology of the Puritans held that deviations from the Way broke the covenant and exposed the entire community to divine retribution.

Nevertheless, Increase strikes a fairly new, and somewhat

desperate note, occasioned by the "Plenty" of "our Peace," new fashions and habits, and the slighting of the established class structure. In other words, the journey through an alleged wilderness by plain, "medieval" villagers confronts prosperity, urbanity, and social fluidity. Everything Increase says is good Platonic doctrine; but it also represents a reactionary "queerness" in Puritanism on the one hand, and the Puritans' becoming swept up in this-worldly preoccupation on the other. If Puritans were not leaving their solitary sojourn to indulge in temporal delights, they were leaving it to concern themselves with others' leaving it. Either way, they tended to lose sight of the otherworldly destination. Sometime later, when the "Puritan" religion became a matter of external prohibitions instead of an inner approach to the peace that passeth understanding, the Platonic pilgrimage had come virtually to an end.

THE VERY APPEARANCE of certainty in Puritanism makes that certainty suspect. The Puritan tendency to split every last hair in exposition of Scripture suggests a desperate effort to win a certainty not fully felt even in the early days of 1630. The gnawing doubts might indicate a subsiding of the original Puritan impulse, but Puritanism itself could have been called forth as an overcompensating defense of a faith that was waning, as of a way of life that was passing.

Men like Shepard had a hard time accepting the faith in the first place, and John Cotton long resisted it as an encumbrance. But their hardest time would have come with a reversion to doubt *after* accepting it and committing their lives to it. Did the decision to build a house elsewhere than on the sands of this world amount to building an aircastle? One of Shepard's mentors, the then-famous Thomas Goodwin, said around 1628 that the elect are as prone to distrust as the damned are to hope, the needle of their souls veering as far toward hell as that of the others toward heaven.[136] Doubt, in any case, meant a distrust of one's own earlier judgment in undertaking the pilgrimage, as well as a sense of guilt at possibly betraying God after once contracting with Him.

Shepard knew such post-covenant doubts. He said 24 November 1641:

I felt over Night *much Darkness and Unbelief;* and saw, that if Satan had once made us begin to doubt, he would hold us with Doubts continually, about the Being of God and Truth of the Scriptures.[137]

Cotton Mather's old preacher friend John Baily said on one occasion in his diary: "I was almost in the *Suburbs of Hell* all day; a meer *Magor* missabib," and on another occasion: "I have been many a Time ready to give up all, and lay down my Ministry, thinking that God had utterly forsaken me .... But by the consideration of the *Brazen Serpent*, I was somewhat Recovered."[138]

Edwards feared he would doubt. In May 1724 he took precautions against any future time when he might incline to turn from the Congregational Way.[139] Much of his regimen seems to have been a steeling against threatening doubt. Certainly he must have been conditioned in some degree by the widespread doubt of others about him. His grandfather Stoddard had perceived that "There is abundance of atheism in the hearts of men .... And .... some godly men are much exercised with this temptation ...." Stoddard sounds as though he were directly counseling his young grandson, who had such difficulty achieving an "authentic" conversion and complained of regressive dullness. Stoddard counsels in pilgrim metaphors: After the converted person "has had affection and inlargements *for a while,* he is wont to complain that he *grows more dull,* and he is afraid that his Convictions are about to leave him .... So men in a Journey, have sometimes good way, sometimes bad; they meet with Rivers and miery places, where they cannot make "speed."[140]

The increasing virulence of 17th-century New England suppression of heresy looks suspiciously like a growing doubt of the Puritan position by Puritans. The victory over Antinomianism cost them heavily. Edward Johnson's depressed state of mind, which he describes in his *Wonder-Working Providence of Sions Saviour, evidently* stemmed from deep doubts regarding orthodoxy.[141] Winthrop, who seemed so sure of his position throughout the crisis, had to review the foundations of his belief, and that meant a pensive critique of his entire life—the same thing Shepard went through about the same time. Winthrop did not behave like a victorious champion when his side won and he swept decisively back into the chief magistracy. The doctrine of free justification, as he calls it, "brought me as low (in my owne apprehension) as if the whole work had been to begin anew."

But when the voice of peace came, I knew it to bee the same that I had been acquainted with before, though it did not speak so loud nor in that measure of joy that I had felt sometimes.[142]

Winthrop sounds something like Ann Bradstreet, who says: "I have often been perplexed that I have not found that joy in my pilgrimage and refreshing which I supposed most of the Servants of God have ...." Her childhood and adolescent experience had been similar to Winthrop's, Bradford's, and many other Puritans': she says she found much comfort in reading the Scriptures in her childhood, also much trouble mending her disobedient and lying childish ways, and much sickness. Smallpox at sixteen brought her around to religion again. She married Simon Bradstreet, and on the flagship with Winthrop came to America,

Where I found a new World and new manners at which my heart rose, But after I was convinced it was the way of God, I submitted to it and joined to the Church at Boston.—After some time I fell into a lingering sickness like a consumption together with a lameness—which correction I saw the lord sent to humble me and do me good .... he hath never suffered me long to sit loose from him, but by one affliction or other hath made me look home, and search what was amiss ... I have no sooner felt my heart out of order, but I have expected, correction for it, which most commonly hath been upon my own person, in sickness weakness and pains, sometimes on my soul in doubts, and fears of Gods displeasure, and my sincerity towards him.

Her struggle to reconcile herself to the American wilderness and to keep going despite distressing illness (much of it apparently psychoneurotic) was at the same time a struggle against unbelief.

Many times hath Satan troubled me concerning the verity of the scriptures, many times by Athiesim, and how I could know weither there was a God, I never saw any miracles to confirm me, and those which I read of, how did I know but they were feigned. That there is a God my reason would tell me, by the wounderous works that I see, the vast frame of the Heavens and Earth, the order of all things Night and Day, Summer and Winter, Spring and Autumn, the dayly providing for this great houshold upon the earth, the preserving and directing of all to its proper End.[143]

Her poem on the death of her one-and-a-half-year-old grand-child Elizabeth in 1665 shows deep outrage and questioning of Providence, but the last line dutifully says what is supposed to be said:

> *By nature Trees do rot when they are grown.*
> *And Plumbs and Apples throughly ripe do fall,*
> *And Corn and grass in their season mown,*
> *And time brings down what is both strong and tall*
> *But plants new set to be eradicate,*
> *And buds new blown, to have so short a date,*
> *Is by his hand alone that guides nature and fate.*[144]

Increase Mather records his own struggle with atheistical thoughts during his early pastorate:

> Soon after my ordination I was grievously molested with temptations to atheism, whereby my spirit was much afflicted and broken . . . . The special thing that satisfied me was that I had experience of great answers of prayer, whereby I could but see that there is a God, and that he is rewarder of them that diligently seek him.[145]

Knowing well what it was to doubt, Increase declaimed during the crisis of King Philip's War: *"Give not way to desperate un-believing thoughts . . . ."* At first, he says, "we too much de-spised the chastning of the Lord, let us not now faint when we are rebuked of him: we are apt to run into extreams."[146] But it is Increase of all the leading Puritans who died the bitterest death. He had said that he believed in God because his prayers were answered. The fervent prayer of many years that he might go back to England remained, however, unanswered. When he realized 17 June 1715 that it never would be answered, he spoke in his *Autobiography* as though his life had closed on that date. (He lived eight years longer.) At the end, in the agony of death by the stone—Judge Sewall tells of hearing him yell out "Pity me! Pity me!"[147]—he doubted the worth of everything he had ever done or lived for and, as his son Cotton says, his head ran much "upon the Horror of being *Deceived at the last*."[148] But Cotton, who always did his duty as he saw it, managed at the final moment to get his father to say he did believe as he expired in Cotton's arms.

Yet Cotton had gone through the same doubts and faced the 18th century with a more precarious sense of security than his father could have fathomed. "My life has been strangely filled with Temptations," says Cotton in his diary in March 1709. "But I heve been lately Tempted with a *new Assault* from Hell, violently made upon me. I am assaulted with Sollicitations to look upon the whole *Christian Religion,* as —————— (I dare not mention, what!) ...."[149] Only Cotton Mather would have had long passages from one of his own books (*Restitutus*) read to him the day before he died. (The day before he died was his 65th birthday.) His son Samuel, who did the reading, reports that Cotton had a *"sweet Composure and easy Departure."*[150]

Doubt had, of course, always plagued Christianity; yet it had grown progressively devastating from the time Thomas Aquinas felt obliged to prove the existence of God. Doubt intensified Puritan anxiety precisely because the Puritans refused to succumb to it (i.e. to the Devil, as they said). Others might be able to relax in agnosticism or pantheism, but Puritans—while they remained definable as such—could not relinquish an otherworldly commitment without subverting the foundation of their mental economy. The strenuousness of their commitment indicates its importance to their sanity as, by the same token, doubt posed so much the greater threat to it. The threat was increasingly acute because doubt was increasingly widespread.

IF PURITANISM were a mental disease, it would have borne some direct relationship to the wringing prevalence of physical disease in the 17th and 18th centuries. The Puritan children's verse,

> Come, let us now forget our mirth,
> And think that we must die,

reminds us of the repeated bereavement of families. "Be not so set upon your childish play," Cotton Mather adressed the Latin-School students at the funeral of their principal, Ezekiel Cheever.

Children, it is your dawning time.—It may be your dying time. —It is now upon computation found, that more than half the children of men die before they come to be seventeen years of age.[151]

Mather, who was always kind and gentle to children, was not just being a morbid Puritan preacher, even though Puritanism cultivated the idea of death as destination, therefore as preoccupation. He was simply facing the staggering statistics he cites.

Infection and exposure at birth took a heavy toll of the 50% who died before the age of seventeen. Thereafter the biggest killers were: tuberculoisis (Jonathan Edwards lost his daughter Jerusha and Cotton Mather his daughter Katy from tuberculosis); smallpox (John Cotton lost his eldest daughter and youngest son in the smallpox epidemic of 1649); bacillary dysentery (the "bloody flux," which probably caused the wholesale loss of life of 1630 and in military camps during most of the wars; Mrs. Jonathan Edwards died of it in Philadelphia, October 1758); diphtheria (the "throat distemper," such as slaughtered half the children in many villages near the time of the Great Awakening): scarlet fever (two daughters and a son of Cotton Mather caught this but did not die, in 1704; they had survived smallpox in 1702); and, strangely, measles.[152]

In the measles epidemic of the fall of 1713 Mather lost his wife, his new-born twins, two small daughters, a son, and a maid. His wife Elizabeth died first, November 9, and his youngest daughter Jerusha, "my pretty little Daughter," "a marvellous witty, ready, forward Child," last, on November 21. Between 9 and 10 (presumably a.m.), he says,

my lovely *Jerusha* Expired. She was two years, and about seven Months, old. Just before she died, she asked me to pray with her . . . . My poor Family is now left without any Infant in it, or any under seven Years of age.[153]

December 6 he writes: "My life is almost a continual Conversation with Heaven . . . ."[154] His third wife went insane, and finally his wayward son Increase ("Cresy") who had given him constant distress, drowned in a shipwreck in August 1724.

. . . I am now advised, that my Son *Increase,* is lost, is dead, is gone . . . . Ah! My Son *Increase!* My Son! My Son!
My Head is Waters, and my Eyes are a Fountain of Tears! I am overwhelmed! . . . .[155]

The boy's grandfather and godfather, Increase, had had his

worst days worrying about seriously sick children. He records in his diary that a son, Nathaniel, took ill the morning of 5 April 1675 with vomiting, gripings, and worms. Increase sat up all night with him. Toward morning the fever and pains abated, but Increase could not get much work done on his sermon. Nathaniel had improved by the 8th, but during the night of the 9th Samuel came down very ill and Nathaniel had grown worse. "Little doe children think, what affection is in the Heart of a Father," increase wrote. He wept and prayed for Sam's life and applied salad oil and a "clyster," and Sam mended. The parents and their eldest son Cotton prayed and wept together for the lives of the two sick children, following a day of fasting and humiliaton on Increase's part. Increase pathetically used such arguments in his prayers as the desirability of keeping up the name of his deceased brother Samuel, an especially blessed minister, and the fact that both boys had been given to the Lord at their birth (by baptism), so were the *Lord's* children, not just his own. Nathaniel kept riviving and relapsing until the 20th, when his fever finally broke.[156] He grew into a saintly youth, surviving with hookworm to the age of twenty. Samuel nearly died of smallpox—and of being bled of seven ounces of blood —in London about two years after Nathaniel's death in Boston.

The poet-preacher contemporary of Increase and Cotton Mather, the slight, wiry, grave, quick-reacting Edward Taylor of Westfield, wrote a heartbreaking poem, *Vpon Wedlock, and Death of Children,* around 1685, recounting the death of three of his children.

> *But oh! the torture, Vomit, Screechings, groans,*
> *And Six weeks Fever would pierce hearts like Stones.*[157]

The colonists did not need Puritanism to account for the shroud they lived under.

PURITANISM was not the disease, but the resiliency that could find strength to go on despite disease—the disease of an unjust world. Puritanism enabled Taylor to rise above the grief and futility of his drab daily life and ask:

> *What Love is this of thine, that Cannot bee*
> *In thine Infinity, O Lord, Confinde . . .?*[158]

A sense of majesty buoys the mighty *Magnalia Christi Americana.* "I WRITE the *Wonders* of the CHRISTIAN RELIGION," Mather opens it, "wherewith His Divine Providence hath *Irradiated* an *Indian Wilderness.*"[159] The majestick & awful Voice of God's Thunder" led Edwards, who said his heart was ready to break for the longing it had, to "sweet Contemplations of my great and glorious GOD."[160] In the end, the quiet grandeur of the pilgrim aspiration somehow triumphed over the bereavement and despair that prompted it. "Shall not thy golden gleams run through this gloom?" asks Taylor in February 1684;

> .... *Shine forth, bright sun: arise*
> *Enthrone thy Rosy-Selfe within mine Eyes.*[161]

Chapter 5

A Pilgrim in Vanity Fair

We are travelling through a malicious, a calumnious, and abusive world ....
—COTTON MATHER, *Bonifacius*, 1710

... The more Christian a man is, the more evils, sufferings and deaths is he made subject to ....
—MARTIN LUTHER, *Treatise on Christian Liberty*, 1520

RICHARD MATHER'S son and John Cotton's daughter ought to have made a terrific genetical combination, and their first child, born in John Cotton's solitary house on a hill in Boston, did for a fact turn out to be a prodigy extraordinary. That is not exactly why we have to consider Cotton Mather as a pilgrim case study, but his mental gifts did much to make him the uncontested leader of the clergy in his time and to give him the clearest perception of anybody of the moral peril Puritanism faced in the new age a-dawning. The dilemma caught him the most cruelly, with his fidelity to the values of his fathers and his acute awareness of the modern tendencies that seemed to doom them.

The critical pivotal time into which he was born, therefore, could be said to account for his inner disturbance. But perhaps an equal factor was that he all but burst with a personal ambition to match his prodigious mind, while the kind of honor to which he aspired no longer received general recognition as the highest, or even as an uncompromised honor, particularly in his own metropolitan Vanity Fair. We have here the elements of a life of complete frustration and failure, and also of a peronality that could be seen—was seen even in his own day—as comical.

But the last chapter takes a surprising turn. Mather's devotion to his cause and his country triumphs over all selfish considerations. He does not turn bitter or vindictive; he does not crack up; he does not succumb to the times; and he does not fail. He actually finds the way to save Puritanism and charge it with new vitality. Grief, age, anxiety, isolation, mistakes, public abuse, and being thrown totally upon his own resources, finally near the end force a touch of greatness upon what would otherwise have been a mere prodigy.

The Cotton Mather who looks out from Peter Pelham's mezzotint is not a nervous or ascetic-looking type, but more like a calm, kind, substantial judge—periwigged. He handled a great multiplicity of tasks ably. To his contemporaries he did not appear the restless, anxious, furtive egotist he does in his diaries. Only the tremendous volume of his production and the incredible number of his activities might have betrayed such to his contemporaries. These things and his stammering. But one of his great triumphs was overcoming that.

His excellent biographer, Barrett Wendell, speaks of Mather's overworked, overwrought habits of life and of his hot temper and quick tongue.[162] Cotton bawled Judge Sewall out in public one day for treating his father, Increase, worse, he said, than a Negro. But all in all, Cotton is more notable for holding his tongue and for working constantly, in semi-seclusion. "No native of this country, as I imagine, had read so much, or retained more of what he had read," the implacable old Charles Chauncy told Ezra Stiles. "He was the greatest redeemer of time I ever knew . . . ."[163] By the age of twelve he could read Virgil, Homer, and the New Testament in their original languages, and before the age of 14 (while at Harvard) he "composed *Hebrew* Exercises, and *Ran* thro the other Sciences, that *Academical Students* ordinarily fall upon. . . ."[164] It is truly remarkable that he could write in time in seven languages and that his works include one each in Spanish, French, and Iroquois.

He published the appalling number of 300 volumes, including the tremendous *Magnalia* with its spate of invaluable, cleverly-written biographies and historical essays. (His bulky auto-biography and his *Biblia Americana*, by far the biggest book he wrote, remain today unpublished.)

Yet all this shows a furtiveness too, as though he worked compulsively in great haste to keep from pondering the basic predicament of himself and Puritanism. "Much *ACTIVITY* in Christianity, this will argue the *Strength* of it; this will declare the Christian to be a *strong Man*; one *strong* in Grace . . . ."[165] Or so Mather rationalized. At the beginning of his autobiography he quotes a passage from an anonymous book he liked: "All such as are Renewed, have an inward principle of a *Divine Life* in them" which, among other things, encourages the methods and ways "that may lead to an HIGH PITCH in those practices."

His much activity and high pitch, however, were directed rather exclusively to his own glory. *"But the Time for Favour was now come . . . !"* he exults in April 1692 at the return of his father with the new provincial charter. (He says this immediately after anticipating a *"speedy Death"* and blessing God that he could die.)

. . . Instead, of my being made a Sacrifice to wicked *Rulers*, all the *Councellours* of the Province, are of my own Father's Nomination; and my *Father-in-Law*, with several *related* unto mee, and several *Brethren* of my own church, are among them. The *Governour* [Sir William Phipps] . . . is . . . one whom I baptised . . . one of my own *Flock*, and one of my dearest Friends.[166]

In point of fact, the new charter virtually ended the clergy's role as rallyers of the people against oppressive rulers, as well as confirming the clergy's permanent removal from any real political power. The following March, aged 31, Cotton said: "I do now beleeve, that some *great Things* are to bee done for mee, by the *Angels* of God."[167] Instead, a son was born March 28 with an accluded rectum and died in agony April 1. Mather's fame-hungering book on the witch trials, published in this period when the reaction to them had set in, discredited him with a dreadful finality among a significant segment of the public, especially in Boston. Pursuing every avenue to eminence but with either limited success or miserable failure, his quest took on desperation.

And I did also for the most part every Day, take Time extraordinary, to cast myself prostrate on my Study floor, and cry to the Lord from the Dust, that His Pardoning, Praeserving, directing Mercies, might not be withheld from me.[168]

Now to be self-seeking is not in itself neurotic. That is all too normal. The feeling that everything was being lost and going wrong may not have been abnormal. That is all too realistic. But his heroically fighting the good fight for Puritanism, alone as he thought, with nobody to turn to but himself, and the feeling that the whole fight was by inheritance and position his personal responsibility, verge on more than selfish, realistic, modern individualism.

Mather himself records the change that began to come over him during his 41st year. "Before the late weeks of my Life," he says in January 1703, "I had rarely known any Tears, except those that were for the Joy of the Salvation of God. But now, scarce a Day passes me without a Flood of Tears, and my Eyes even decay with weeping."[169] Gradually he developed a disinterested commitment to service, and a kind of noble resignation. His *Essays to Do Good* reflects his own rising above personal resentment, party wrangling, and of class and time, with that same disposition to compose and harmonize in the interests of a higher purpose that characterizes Penn, Franklin, and Jefferson. "We may be unjustly defamed," Mather writes; "it will be strange if we are not frequently so." But instead of flying into a rage when reproached, we should patiently inquire whther God is not thus awaking us to some duty. "You must accept of any public service, of which you are capable"; and there is nothing to compare with "the Ravishing Satisfaction" of "relieving the Distresses of a Poor, Mean, *Miserable Neighbour*" or "in doing any *Extensive Service* for the Kingdom of our Great SAVIOUR in the World; or any thing to redress the Miseries under which Mankind is generally Languishing." But "To *Do Well*, and to *Hear Ill*, is the Common Experience, and ought to be our Constant Expectation." You must be above all discouragements. "Look for them, and with a magnanimous *Courage* overlook them."[170]

WITH ALL THEIR STRIVING for Augustinian ecstasy, the Puritans of the prime were no dreamy hermits. Even Kelpius came out of his cave to teach, garden, and practice medicine. Winthrop, who felt as concerned as Plato for the commonwealth, worked in shirtsleeves alongside servants and hired laborers in the first few founding years. A good symbol of the Puritans' combined contemplative and active life would be the books and six pair of spectacles next to carpentry tools in Winthrop's den that passed equally for a study and a workshop. Edwards and Shepard took as active a concern as Augustine in the administration of church and community; ministers like Stoddard and Hooker seem to have controlled both. William says he wrought hard at the hoe for his bread while a preacher in Plymouth and Salem. He doubtless did much of the building of his own frame house in Providence, turned trader and, whenever occasion required, served as Indian diplomat, magistrate, arbiter, and overseas agent. Bradford and Brewster found ways to cope with every kind of practical exigency, including scurvy, exposure, famine, staggering debt, subversion, trade competition, Indian conspiracy, etc. and never defaulted in their responsibility.

Increase Mather administered Harvard College and, with Cotton, a church of a thousand members; became a popular hero by calling for resistance (which was in vain) to giving up the revoked charter of the colony; salvaged the lower house of the Bay's self-government while nominally representing the Bay churches in England; organized the clergy on his return and led them in putting enough pressure on the Governor and Council that these magistrates directed the Court of Oyer and Terminer to throw spectral evidence out of the witch trials and so brought that delusion to an end;[171] and he and Cotton, both of whom proved to be ardent patriots during and after the Revolution of 1689, got hopelessly mixed up in all the public affairs of their colony, notwithstanding their constant sessions of solitary prayer and all-night vigils. These pilgrims could say with Seneca, a supremely favorite author of theirs, that one reason for shutting themselves up was to help a greater number.

Cotton could say this, at least from the time of turning 41— which was not long after the turn of the century. But he had come to maturity during that Puritan-backbreaking transition when the civil government ceased to consult the clergy on momentous issues, and the public at large ceased to grant them the status of oracles. Mather could advance the public welfare merely as a minister of a private church, and as a private citizen without portfolio. His agitated intensity therefore sprang in part from a closer confinement of an undiminished need to act. It was in something of a hand-wringing state that he felt the old Puritan impulse to bring people up out of their cave to the light, to reform and redeem. ("And this work of reformation is the great business of every man while he lives," Plato said in *The Laws*. "Speaking generally, our glory is to follow the better and improve the inferior.")

Cotton cut through the thickening layers of insulation that threatened to seal him off from the world he longed to make a great impact upon, by the little clubs he initiated which he called Reforming Societies. These private organizations, depending on neither church nor state, furthered such projects as better manners, charity, and good civic works in general—all to mobilze public opinion on the side of piety, reestablish a bygone unity, and provide for the maximum longevity of Puritanism in the teeth of modern times.[172]

He also seized on science as a way to get through to society at large and change it. His plumping for mass smallpox inoculations—before he had any scientific verification to warrant them—is his most celebrated success in exploiting "science" for his and God's glory and the incalculable benefit of mankind. Cotton pleated for *practical* measures to "redress the Miseries under which Mankind is generally Languishing"; he moved energetically to leaven the inert philistinism of his region; and he dearly wanted to wield a universal influence beyond furthering nicer manners and assisting in the improvement of congregational singing, etc. The appeal of the Puritans' adored Ramaean logic, after all, was its purpose of using or applying knowledge, un-Platonic though that may sound. The intention of getting results, by clearer knowledge of the nature of reality and a more efficient use of this knowledge, helps explain why Puritanism embraced (or thought it embraced) science. No more than Plato or Thomas Aquinas (who synthesized Aristotle and Augustine) did Puritans give up a basic insistence on reason and on seeing things exactly as they were. Even while remaining immersed in the medieval academic habits of the *trivium* and *quadrivium*, which perpetuated classical theoretical science, Puritanism tended to be pragmatic.

One of the most widely informed men in natural science as then known, Cotton Mather advocated a joining of religion and science—or "philosophy" as they called it then. Such a juncture, he calculated, would convert an insidious threat, already undermining the old Puritanism, into a lifesaving ally. *"Philosophy* is no *Enemy*," he protests in one of his swan-song works, *The Christian Philosopher*, "but a mighty and wondrous *Incentive to Religion*." He deliberately chooses and stresses the term "a PHILOSOPHICAL RELIGION."[173]

Practicing what he preached, he had expended years of heavy toil on gargantuan exegesis of the Bible "agreable to the Modern Discoveries": the *Biblia Americana*. In it he partially rearranges the books and chapters of the Bible into what he regards as a chronological history, and paraphrases and explicates the whole in the light and ostensibly in the spirit of the new science. He, for instance, has a long, erudite discussion of gravity, vacuum, diurnal rotation, and parabolic ellipses in relation to the account of creation in *Genesis*. He applies his coldly logical technique and comes up with such mathematically-undisputable facts as that there are 23,205 verses in the Old Testament and 7,956 in the New. He makes such further exact calculations as that "From the Autumnal Equinox next after the Creation of *Adam*, to that at the End of the Deluge," equals a span of 1,656 years and no months and, fortunately, "There are no Considerable Difficulties in this period." His modern scientific temper allows him to re-read the Scriptures as reasonable, common-sense narratives. For example:

> *Adam* was no doubt, throughly instructed by his maker, in the History of the World, & his own Creation. And since *Methusela* was above two hundred & forty years old before the Death of *Adam*, how easily might those be from him, received and preserved among the Antediluvian patriarchs . . . !

In the fourth manuscript volume Mather inserts an appendix to the book of *Acts* that includes an erudite history of the Jews and a 1697 "scientific" pamphlet on *Eating of Blood*. The final volume concludes in Mather's grand manner with thirteen appendices in the form of scientific treatises, ranging from comparative weights, measures, and coins, to the Second Coming. The conclusion of the text proper is "An Essay, for a further Commentary, on the Sacred Scriptures":

> We have call'd in the Help of all *Sciences*, and *Histories*, to Illustrate the *Oracles* of God. But we will now repair to another Fountain of *Illustrations*, which we may find in the EXPERIENCE of the Faithful.

In line with his idea of a philosophical religion, he here calls for Experimental Christians, i.e. pious persons who will observe and record what they observe in their own inner lives, to confirm the truth of Scripture. "In the *observations* of *Experimental Christians,* we should have notable and glorious *Expositions* of many Things contained in the *Book of Truth . . . .*"

Mather does not go very far in the first volume of the *Biblia Americana* before ringing in the pilgrim theme. William Harvey's work on generation is the point of departure; for Harvey seems to confirm that the soul is carried into the womb in the male seed; and the evident fact that the embryo remains unfastened to the mother by any ligaments for at least the first three months, further attests a transfer of the soul from elsewhere into an alien environment.

In what part of the *Body* soever, the *Soul* may have its principal seat, which is variously disputed, it is most certainly no other than a *Foreigner* and a *Sojourner* here, and placed by god in this Earthly Tabernacle, for a certain Term; upon the Expiration of which Term, it should go back, to its *heavenly Countrey;* even the Countrey which *Plato* acknowledged, when he called it . . . *That Super-coelestial place . . . .*[174]

One of Mather's severest disappointments was his failure to find anyone who would publish the *Biblia Americana;* and one of his most flaunted prides was putting "F.R.S." after his name when he had been admitted to membership in the Royal Society, Sir Isaac Newton president. But the central motivation of his scientific enthusiasm was not very scientific. It was a defensive, *a priori* determination to confirm the truth of the Book of Truth; it was an urgent, dammed-up desire to inflame piety, charity, good will, and evangelism: to answer the grand end of being, which Mather reminds us is "To glorify GOD."

With all his energy and ability, Mather was left to pursue this grand end mostly indoors, alone and in silence, resigned to doing well and hearing evil.

His MOOD OF RESIGNATION, combined with a resolve to strive on, colors his autobiography, entitled *Paterna.* Two Biblical quotations on the opening page are especially revealing: *Job* 9. 21: "Tho' I were perfect,—yett would I despise my Life." And Psalm 119. 74: "They that Fear thee will be glad when they see me; because I have believed in thy word!"

There is a dignity in his last books, born of the silent, solitary walking on in his chosen course regardless. He busied himself with constant secret charities and rose to the height of judging other people, especially enemies and wrongdoers, with a charity his father never managed. At length, nervously exhausted, grief-drained, bleak-feeling, he penned his final diary entry, 7 February 1725:

> When I sitt alone in my Languishments, unable to write, or to read, I often compose little Hymns, and sing them unto the Lord . . . .
> Having found my Mind for some time without such precious and impressive Thoughts of GOD my SAVIOUR, as are the Life of my Spirit, I . . . mourn'd and sang unto the Lord . . . .[175]

In the last sermon he preached—a funeral sermon for his pastor friend at Milton, Peter Thatcher, who died 17 December 1727—Cotton followed Tertullian in interpreting *Isaiah* 26. 20 —"Come, my People, Enter thou into my Chambers"—as an invitation to die readily and cheerfully.[176] Walking toward the roar of the river, Cotton accepted this invitation.

Chapter 6

The Big Switch

The times are not always alike; it is a world of
Change that we live in . . . .
—SAMUEL WILLARD, *The Peril of the Times*,
1700

We live in a World of Change . . . where a little
Time, a few Revolutions of the Sun, brings to
pass strange Things, surprizing Alterations . . . .
—JONATHAN EDWARDS, *Farewell Sermon*, 1750

BENJAMIN FRANKLIN could not properly be called a pilgrim,
though he took early delight in Bunyan's works, as he notes in
his *Autobiography*. The *Autobiography* is as much a pre-
scription for success in this world as *Poor Richard's Almanack*.
It has even been interpreted as a secular *Pilgrim's Progress*.[177]
But this all the more underscores the switch from a heavenly-
city destination.

A prayer Franklin wrote at the age of 22—"O Creator, O
Father, I believe . . . . that thou art *pleas'd with the Pleasure* of
thy Children"— gives away his belief that pleasure in this world
takes precedence over pleasure in the next.[178] H preferred to
stay and make the most of the wilderness rather than just pass
through grimly enduring it, and complacently told the young

evangelist George Whitefield that he expected the Lord would take care of him according to his deserts in the next world as in this.

So he became a rogue of great practical value in innumerable ways, a man of humor, charm, warmth, and worldliness—an honor to human nature, Jefferson said. Yet he went about his quest for success and development of personality with a very Puritan love of learning, acquired in Boston. After founding the Philadelphia library, he tells us, he became its best customer. In 1724, before taking final leave of Boston, he had called on the most voracious reader and encourager of science of the time, the ageing Cotton Mather. Bidding Mather goodbye, he bumped his head on a low beam; whereat Mather advised him to do a little judicious stooping now and then. Franklin did learn the art of lowering-of-self, in time. He also took to heart Mather's appeal i nthe *Essays to Do Good*:

Awake, Shake off thy Shackles, ly no longer fettered in a Base confinement unto nothing but a Meaner Sort of Business. Assume and Assert the Liberty of now and then Thinking on the *Noblest Question* in the World; *What Good may I do in the World?"* [179]

Franklin became about the best do-gooder yet. As a famous old man he wrote Mather's son Samuel from Passy 10 November 1779 that he had met with the *Essays to Do Good* when a boy, and it "gave me such a turn of thinking, as to have an influence on my conduct through life; for I have always set a greater value on the character of a doer of good than any other kind of reputation."[180]

In the year of the first edition of Mather's *Essays*—1710— a poem went the rounds mocking the celebrated clergyman's prolific publishing and his getting a doctor's degree:

> *The mad enthusiast, thirsting after fame,*
> *By endless volum'ns thought to raise a name ....*
> *Parkhurst says, Satis fecisti,*
> *My belly's full of your Magnalia Christi.*[181]

The young leather-aproned apprentice to a printer brother must have shared these sentiments; they prevailed among the merchants and newspapermen. His own pseudonym, Silence Dogood, is an evident takeoff on Mather.

But notice that Franklin admired his fellow author enough to pay him parting respects and eventually became, himself, the venerable and pious *Dr.* Franklin, learned in all branches of knowledge and universally renowned. In his emphasis on education and on industriousness ("Lose no time," he urges himself in his Thirteen Virtues; "be always employ'd in something useful"), in his devotion to the public interest and public morality, to private societies for social betterment, to writing and publishing, and in being nominally a member of the Presbyterian church in Philadelphia, Franklin perhaps carried more of the Cotton Mather version of Puritanism into Philadelphia than even he suspected. John Adams, at the end of his astute analysis of Frankin, asks a question which would equally apply to Mather:

> What shall we do with these gentlemen of great souls and vast views, who, without the least tincture of vanity, *bonâ fide* believe themselves the greatest men in the world, fully qualified and clearly entitled to govern their governors and command their commanders as well as their equals and inferiors, purely for their good and without the smallest interest for themselves? [182]

But Mather remained, and Franklin ceased to be a pilgrim. We do not know what the two talked about the day Franklin bumped his head at the North Church parsonage. It is easy, however, to imagine Mather addressing Franklin in the following passage Mather tailored in one of his works to the incipient Franklin-type sentiment before Franklin was born:

> You may object, *Yea if I were sure that Heaven were my Home, I should be willing to go.*
> To thee I reply, *Do you make Heaven your Home, and you may be sure it will be so.*[183]

Franklin followed the fashionable trend of his time—not only that of this-worldliness but of the Enlightenment in general: simplifying and standardizing of life thought, minimizing human differences or individual uniqueness, and assuming the universe to be essentially fixed and uncomplicated. It was a period when, as the philosopher Arthur Lovejoy has made impressively clear, the extrovertive God of Plato's *Timaeus* superseded the self-sufficient God of the *Phaedo* and *Republic*. The aspiration to rise from the cave to heaven gave way to an acceptance of one's temporal place in the natural (and static) order of creation and, instead of renouncing this world for the remote Idea of the Good, one revelled in the variety of this tangible world. which variety attested the divinity of a God of overflowing plentitude. God could be called imminent in His creation, and to delight in this world was to glorify the Creator of it.[184]

The American not only found himself at last at home in the wilderness but equal to it. He could see how he had changed the wilderness with his own hands—not as a pawn of supernatural forces but as the active agent itself. This brought him a sense of power and self-confidence, the feeling that he was as worthy of salvation as anyone else and that he could achieve it by his own striving. His experience had fully prepared him to hear the evangelist say, in effect, heaven was his natural right.[185] While American life in four generations had sloughed off manners and grown cruder than it started, the actual physical conditions had grown steadily less harsh, and people could and did turn just as steadily more humanitarian. Thus boorishness and flouting of authority—"I won't worship a wig," one uncouth leveller said with reference to Edwards[186]—could go hand-in-hand with an enhanced mutual respect and concern, one for another. In the theological dispute over church membership and Communion, Edward's congregation would not so much as let him state his own case. But even this rudeness could have come partly from a risen regard for the dignity of individuals as individuals, whether saints or sinners; the congregation felt that this dignity should not properly be challenged by a public test of any kind.

People in ever-larger numbers grew uneasy about any kind of exclusivism, while the people at Northampton acted suspiciously as though they believed everybody had a natural right to belong to the church. Edward's protégé Samuel Hopkins confirms that this was in fact their point of view, in his biography of Edwards published fifteen years after the tragic dismissal. Of late years, says Hopkins, the opinion of Solomon Stoddard (Edwards's grandfather, predecessor, and co-minister) that "persons who have no real goodness, but are in a christless state, and know themselves to be so, may make a christian profession and come to the Sacrament, without lying and hypocrisy; and that they have a right, and 'tis their duty so to do, has greatly spread in the country."[187] Then, as Edwards's great-grandson Sereno Dwight says concerning the crisis at Northampton, it was the *fashion* to belong to the very large church there.[188] The church had grown to about 900 members or more by the close of Edwards's revival of 1735. To make the best of this world and keep an easy conscience, everyone might as well be a gentleman and everybody a saint. And not only did Americans start calling all men, not just magistrates, ministers, and merchants "Mister"; they turned Arminian and went Arminius one better: they decided all men were basically good rather than bad, as well as that they could save themselves if they would.

THE GREAT AWAKENING, which marks the decisive switch in mood, coincided with a revolutionary situation of explosive growth—about 100% increase in population from 1700 to 1740, and well more than 100% in the number of towns in Massachusetts and Connecticut. It also coincided with a ghastly smallpox and diphtheria epidemic, the diphtheria alone killing about 5,000 persons, mostly minors, all over New England in the years 1735-40, often taking half a town's children in a few weeks.[189] The psychological and social upheaval of the time did not require the spread of Newtonian science to materialize, but Newtonian science was nevertheless spreading somewhat like the diphtheria.

Cotton Mather, who coped manfully with Newton, had felt the full brunt of the many simultaneous revolutionary forces— especially those in the economy—a generation before Edwards; because they showed themselves in virulent form in the seaboard metropolis first. The seaboard ministers had a hard time persuading their congregations to the "liberalism" of the Half-Way Covenant, which was a device to allow lukewarm people who had been baptized as infants but who could not honestly profess any subsequent experience of regeneration, to be members of the church but debarred from Communion. On the other hand, Increase Mather's brother Eleazar, the first pastor of the hinterland center Northampton, found himself resisting his congregation's insistence on the Half-Way Covenant, which they finally voted in anyway six months before he died. Some time after the imperious Stoddard succeeded Mather, he went beyond that compromise measure and opened the church to anybody who would come in. This had been the practice at Northampton for seventy years when Edwards decided it should be reversed. To go back to a position that Eleazar Mather had been unable to hold before Stoddard, was to resist both a *de facto* revolution and the further revolution gathering in the present.

The Mathers, in representing the mainline of Puritan orthodoxy, also most faithfully represent the deepest emotional commitment to the Puritan tradition itself. Yet, one of the revolutionary tendencies in American society was rejection of tradition. The ministers Stoddard and John Wise, of Ipswich, in opposing the Mathers within the clergy, were opposing tradition, competing authority, and the city, but not necessarily the idea of a ruling elite, just so they were the elite. Wise, despite being a democrat, had the same knack of forcing clergymen in his neighborhood to conform to his views as Stoddard in the Connecticut Valley.[190] Stoddard exploited frontier independence of Boston and of tradition, but at the same time bossed the Valley as his private empire. "Pope Stoddard," his ineffectual enemies called him: As Pery Miller substantiates, it was the conservative Mathers who kept the democratic element in Puritanism alive.[191] Stoddard went so far as to side with the high-handed Tory governor, Joseph Dudley, whose chief opposition came from the patriot Mathers.[192] With obvious reference to the Mathers in his election sermon in Boston in 1703, Stoddard said that there were many ways whereby persons come to be ill-principled, "some by being too tenacious of old Traditions."[193]

Stoddard held that the pastor alone should determine who was admitted to the church or excommunicated, and was not to be overruled by an "uncapable" congregation. Such matters had always been decided before by the membership at large; for Congregationalism prided itself on its classical "mixt" system of aristocracy and democracy.[194] In upholding the "mixt" system of the first generation, Increase sometimes sounds more anti-democratic than Stoddard. "Another thing which Corrupts the Worship of God," Increase reacted to Stoddard in 1702, "is, *When persons not duely qualified are admitted unto those Ordinances which they have no right unto.*"[195] But Increase never contested the sovereign rights of the membership at large which had duly qualified and been admitted. He announced one day in 1687 that he knew not how to discover the will of God by a vote of the congregation![196]

Increase was indeed more democratic than Stoddard in granting church members their constitutional prerogatives; but in granting membership to all, Stoddard was riding the rising democratic tide. For what people generally were demanding was status, not power. To the popular eye, Mather looked more autocratic than the autocrat Stoddard because Mather maintained a spiritual standard or, as the egalitarians saw it, a social class barrier.

When Edwards reversed Stoddard and returned to the Mather mainline, he did so invoking Stoddard:

'It may possibly be a *Fault* (says Mr. *Stoddard*) to depart from the Ways of our *Fathers:* But it may also be a *Vertue,* and an eminent Act of Obedience, to depart from them in *some* Things. Men are won't to make a great *Noise,* that we are bringing in Innovations, and depart from the *old Way:* But it is beyond me, to find out wherein the *Iniquity* does lie.' [197]

The reversal of Stoddard meant also a painful reversal of Edwards's own earlier sufferance. It was only, Edwards says, "after long searching, pondering, viewing & reviewing, I gain'd Satisfaction, became fully settled in the Opinion I now maintain." He realized that upholding the old orthodoxy might cost him his pulpit, but it is hard to see any wish for martyrdom in his course. "I can truly say . . . 'tis what I engage in with the greatest Reluctance, that ever I undertook any publick Service in my Life. But," he continues, "the State of things with me is so ordered, by the Sovereign Disposal of the Great Governour of the World, that my doing this appeared to me very necessary and altogether unavoidable."[198]

EDWARDS'S STAND on the covenant came out of the old Dissenter view of the church as Christ's embattled vanguard, which must be selective to ensure His victory. For on pledging the covenant, each individual in the church and each individual church as a whole contracted to accept God's proffered grace in return for implicit allegiance to Him.

When attempting to minimize the covenant in Edwards's theology, it is a big fact to overlook that the climactic dismissal from his pulpit occurred over the issue of the covenant, which he insisted on against the will of his congregation. His defense of his position received the backing of the leading Bay ministers Thomas Prince, John Webb, Thomas Foxcroft, and Mather Byles, all of whom signed a preface dated Boston 11 August 1748 attesting that Edwards's was the orthodox conception brought over, as they say, by the judicious fathers of their country from English Puritans and held threescore years without dissension. Edwards reiterates this old concept of the covenant in the context of the flagging zeal of his time:

> . . . *None ought to be admitted to the Privileges of adult Persons in the Church of Christ, but such as make a Profession of real Piety.* For the Covenant, to be owned or profess'd is *God's Covenant,* which he has revealed as the Method of our spiritual Union with him, and our Acceptance as the Objects of his eternal Favour . . . . To own this Covenant, is to profess the Consent of our *Hearts* to it; and that is the Sum and Substance of true Piety . . . .[199]

Through Edwards's big debut sermon in Boston in 1731—*God Glorified in the Work of Redemption*—runs an Augustinian sense of the futility of man, who however has the hope of God's onnipotence as a way to rise above it.

> God hath made Man's Emptiness and Misery, his low, lost and ruin'd State into which he is sunk by the Fall, an Occasion of the greater Advancement of his own Glory . . . . Though God be pleased to lift Man out of that dismal Abyss of Sin and Woe into which he has fallen . . . yet the Creature hath nothing in any Respect to glory of . . . .
> Hence those doctrines and Schemes of Divinity that are in any Respect opposite to such an absolute, & universal Dependance on God, do derogate from God's Glory, and thwart the Design of the Contrivance for our Redemption.[200]

Edwards here seems to have struck his first blow against Arminianism. He unequivocally aligns himself with the old Dissenting tradition against the encroaching modern temper. Sereno Dwight says "The subject was at that time novel . . . . and made a deep impression on the audience."[201] The novelty did not, however, consist in a concealed Lockean meaning; the very opening point of the sermon is that human reason and wisdom do not avail and men must rely completely upon revelation and God:

> The Learned Grecians, and their great Philosophers, by all their Wisdom did not know God, they were not able to find out the Truth in divine Things. But after they had done their utmost to no Effect, it pleased God at length, to reveal himself by the Gospel

which they accounted Foolishness: *He chose the foolish things of the World, to confound the wise . . . .*[202]

The more absolute Edwards could conceive God to be, the more chance he felt of emerging out of earthly impotence and mire. Thus one deep motivation of the original covenant doctrine—to draw closer to the inscrutable and unreachable God, out of a consciousness of man's lowness and need of redemption—precisely motivates Edwards's concept.

The generation of John Cotton, on the other hand, had felt a need to counteract the prevailing overawing conception of God and bring Him down to earth somewhat. As the Puritan flame of that first generation gradually died down, the need arose of re-enthroning a God Who had come to be too familiar, if not taken for granted. It was not the essential doctrine that differed between Cotton and Edwards, but the situation that each encountered with it. The fact is, every major American Puritan from Cotton to Edwards believed in *both God's* illimitable sovereignty *and* His circumscription through the Covenant of Grace, at the same time that they really put love before sovereignty in their theology.

Edwards notes that it took him some time to reach the conclusion of his fathers, but he did, and could finally say:

The Doctrine of God's Sovereignty has very often appeared, an exceeding pleasant, bright and sweet Doctrine to me: and absolute Sovereignty is what I love to ascribe to God.[203]

Yet he also said that "the Godhead or the divine nature and essence does subsist in love";[204] "The Scriptures do represent true Religion, as being summarily comprehended in *Love*, the Chief of the Affections, and Fountain of all other Affections";[205] and "The very quintessence of all Religion, the very thing wherein lies summarily the sincerity, spirituality, and divinity of Religion . . . . is LOVE."[206] Edwards reiterates this idea throughout his works. If love were not the keystone of his theology, the sovereignty of God would more likely have impressed him as "terrifying" than "sweet." In bridging the gap between the terror and the sweetness of God's sovereignty, Edwards abstracts a doctrine which Increase Mather and many another had already built on: "That it is God's manner to make men sensible of their misery and unworthiness, before he appears in his mercy and love to them."[207]

The dispute whether Edwards were the first authentic American Calvinist because he pushed the cushioning covenant aside and went back to the full awful sovereignty of God, loses its savor in the realization that Edwards kept the covenant in place and kept God's sovereignty tempered with love.

Edwards was far from the first American Puritan to emphasize God's sovereignty anyway. His father Timothy said unequivocally, God "is absolutely free and Sovereign";[208] Increase Mather reasserted "the Absolute Sovereignty of God" in a sermon of October 1711;[209] Cotton Mather took pains to repeat what the Cambridge Platform of 1648 had repeated before him, that the churches of New England agreed entirely in doctriine with the Calvinist churches of Europe and the Westminster Confession.[210] Hooker had said that God might dispose one's soul to Hell despite the covenant, but that, regardless, one should be content to be disposed as God wills.[211] Three generations before Edwards, John Cotton had made such statements as "I find, that he that has *Calvin* has them all," and "I love to sweeten my mouth with a piece of *Calvin* before I go to sleep."[212]

As to that sovereignty-doctrine of predestination that the whole covenant idea seems to contradict, Calvin himself did not stand more unqualifiedly for it than William Ames, the acknowledged mentor of the New-England covenant Puritans. Ames effuses in his influential textbook that "predestination hath greatest wisdome, freedome, firmnesse, and immutability joyned with it."[213]

One could not become a Calvinist by pushing aside the cushioning covenant in any case, because Calvin never pushed it aside. "God hath such a souerainty ouer his creatures, as he may dispose of them at his pleasure," Calvin begins a course of 159 sermons on *Job*, but concludes that "we must alwayes be satisfied with life, seeing that God hath giuen vs so good a pledge of his loue in our Lorde Jesus Christ . . . ."[214] Many similar statements of Calvin reflect the cushion of the covenant in his doctrine of sovereignty, notwithstanding that he did not yet feel the later Puritan urge to seize compulsively upon the covenant as a last desperate hope. Throughout his preaching Calvin exudes an undaunted confidence in God's saving grace that American-Puritan preaching does not match. Consider these typical lines (in 16th-century translation) from his course of sermons on *Galatians*:

For fayth doth in suche wyse assure vs of Gods goodnesse, and that the same shal neuer fayle vs . . . . By this Word *Libertie or freedome,* it is meant that we may walke with full confidence before God, and that hee will alwayes be fauorable . . . .[215]

It is true that American Puritanism diverged in letter and spirit in many respects from Calvin, including its greater obsession with the covenant. Covenant-obsession betrays a prior obsession with salvation. It is the preeminent concern for salvation, as Everett Emerson points out, that presents the important difference between the Puritans and Calvin; for Calvin's preeminent concern was God's glory.[216] What ultimately divides American Puritanism from Calvinism, then, is not the presence or absence of the covenant but the increasing degree of modern doubt.

Gene Lavengood suggests that the real first American Calvinist was perhaps Stoddard; for Stoddard departed from Congregational exclusiveness to return to Calvin's church as coterminous with the community. But Stoddard was not even the first Stoddardist. Back in January 1639, one Mrs. Oliver of Salem caused a long commotion by contending that all who dwell in the same town and profess their faith in Christ ought to be received to the sacraments there, and that Paul, were he present in Salem, would call *all* its inhabitants saints.[217]

* * *

GROWING INDIFFERENCE to religion had been saddening the disestablished Congregationalist clergy for two generations before it brought the seething of Edwards. "Lukewarmness in Religion is abominable," he said, at the same time recognizing that its opposite—zeal—"above all other Christian Virtues" needs to be "strictly watched and searched . . . ."[218] Probably the strongest statement Edwards made on any subject was one concerning lukewarmness and the covenant:

Christ came into the World to engage in a War with God's Enemies, *Sin* and *Satan* . . . and the Contest is, who shall have the Possession of OUR HEARTS. Now 'tis reasonable, under these Circumstances, that we should declare on whose Side we are, whether on Christ's Side, or on the Side of his Enemies . . . . If *this* Profession is not made, no Profession is made, that is worth the making . . . . The case admits of no Neutrality, or Lukewarmness . . . . *He that is not with me* (says Christ) *is against me* . . . . To profess no higher Regard to *Christ* than what will admit of a superior Regard to the *World,* is more absurd than if a Woman pretending to marry a Man . . . should profess to take him in some Sort, but yet not pretend to take him in such a Manner as is inconsistent with her allowing other Men a fuller Possession of her . . . .[219]

As Edwards elaborated to his pastor friend Peter Clark of Salem Village, the "great Thing" he scrupled and dared no longer go on in was the people's publicly assenting to the words required for their admission to Communion "without pretending thereby to mean any such Thing as an hearty consent to the Terms of the Gospel Covenant . . . ."

It being, at the same Time that the words are used, Their known & establish'd Principle, which they openly profess & proceed upon, that men may & ought to use these words & mean no such Thing, but something . . . consistent with their knowing That They don't chuse God as their Chief Good, but love the world more than Him, and that They do not give Themselves up entirely to God, but make Reserves . . . .[220]

They mouthed words that had lost their meaning—at a time when Edwards saw New England as engaged in a war for the kingdom of the Lord.[221] *"High-Treason,"* Cotton Mather said, was the crime of those souls now in Hades who followed Satan on earth.[222] Looking round at his unmoved, summer patriots, Edwards recoiled. As Clarence H. Faust detects, Edwards regarded a depraved humanity with loathing.[223]

Their attitude was all the more infuriating in that they had responded hypersensitively to his lashing only a few years before. They had cried out then: "What shall I do to be saved?" A great alteration, as Edwards describes it, came over Northampton, which had not been so free of vice in sixty years. Instead of "revelry, frolicking, profane and licentious conversation, and lewd songs," also "tavern-haunting," the people—particularly the young people; for the Great Awakening was largely a youthful movement—talked seriously of religious things and flocked to religious exercises.[224]

Now the Puritans, from their first colonizing of New England, had the notion of themselves as the saving remnant of true Christianity that would one day re-illumine a darkened world. Cotton Mather's brazen anonymous history of Nonconformity not only reveals how unreconstructed American

Puritanism remained near the turn of the century, it obliviously heralds "a more glorious Reformation and Revolution at hand."[225] Edwards entertained great hopes that the spreading revival he initiated in Northampton was nothing less than the long-awaited re-illumination:

> 'Tis not unlikely that this Work of God's Spirit . . . is the Dawning, or, at least, a Prelude of that glorious Work of God, so often foretold in Scripture, which . . . shall renew the World of Mankind . . . . And there are many Things that make it probable that this Work will begin in *America*.[226]

Astonishing as was the longevity of revival intensity at Northampton, it inevitably ebbed in three or four years; then Whitefield's visit reanimated it. When the second, irreversible ebb was setting in, Edwards insisted more stubbornly than ever: "The Things of Religion take place in Mens Hearts, no further than they are *affected* with them."[227] Only when the revival was dead in Northampton did Edwards's construction of the covenant get strict.

* * *

THE REASON for his strict constructionism was the same as his reason for stimulating the great revival in the first place: apathy and complacency. When he voiced his contempt of the Pharisees as "Patterns of Hypocrisy" during the first ebb of his revival in a lecture-sermon of October 1740, he surely had his own listeners in mind. He took as the text on this occasion, *Matthew* 5.20: "For I say unto you that Except your Righteousness shall Exceed the Righteousness of the scribes & Pharisees ye shall in no case enter into the Kingdom of Heaven." One special design of the Sermon on the Mount, he proceeded to say, was to correct the errors, doctrine, and practice of the Pharisees; which, transparently, is the design of his own sermon with respect to the errors, doctrine, and practice of his pharisaical flock. Statements of his in subsequent years about outward show of religion without real piety on the part of his communicants, leave little doubt as to the conscious analogy in his mind between these communicants and the Pharisees. He repeated this lecture-sermon January 1753 (with a trace of vindictiveness?) when the Great Awakening was over and he had been a year and a half in exile from Northampton.[228]

The stakes of eternity were so high, the crisis of salvation so urgent—or rather, the indifference to them had grown so great —that Edwards did not scruple to scare if he could, any more than he would hesitate, as he said, "to fright a person out of a house on fire."[229]

If there be really a Hell of such dreadful, and never ending Torments, as is generally supposed [Edwards said], that Multitudes are in great Danger of, and that the bigger Part of Men in Christian Countries do actually from Generation to Generation fall into . . . for want of taking due care to avoid it; then why is it not proper for those that have the Care of Souls, to take great Pains to make Men sensible of it? Why should not they be told as much of the Truth as can be? [230]

The incidence of the scare technique jumped during times of crisis; but overall, it increased in proportion as otherworldliness waned, and the resort to fire and brimstone at last became prevalent in the period of the Great Awakening. Michael Wigglesworth did not produce the 224 morbid stanzas of his popular poem *The Day of Doom* in the vigorous prime of Puritanism but in 1662, the very year that the Half-Way Covenant gave regretful official recognition to the religious stupor that had grown great enough to menace control of the holy commonwealth by church members. When hell had been generally more terrifying, preachers had no great need to invoke its terror often; just as when revival enthusiasm stayed lively, Edwards had no great need to insist on sincerity and wholeheartedness in professing the covenant. When people grew balkier about the other world, they came under desperate clergical flagellation, and they responded as though pain-maddened, for awhile.

In the first generation in Puritan Massachusetts, some member or other of Shepard's congregation would cry out in agony during his sermons (according to the memory of them preserved in the 18th century): "what shall I do to be saved?" Though Shepard kept his voice low, his preaching was remembered as so searching "as a hypocrite could not easily bear it, and it seemed irresistible."[231] Shepard preached this way following the Antinomian convulsion, which saw the first concerted challenge to clerical authority and Congregational orthodoxy and which coincided with an Indian War, a severe economic depression, sudden expansion of territory and population, an unleashed greed for land and worldly vices, and an alarming egalitarian spirit—as when Mary Winthrop Dudley's maid, on being bade to do something, told her mistress to do it herself. This early, Shepard felt it his duty to revive a slipping faith. He even preached a close equivalent of Edwards's long-later scare sermon, *The Future Punishment of the Wicked Unavoidable and Intolerable.* "What cares God for a vile wretch, whom nothing can make good while it lives?" Shepard accused. "Thou canst not endure the torments of a little Kitchin fire on the tip of thy finger, not one half hour together; how wilt thou bear the fury of this infinite, endless, consuming fire in body and soul throughout all eternity?"[232]

"What a dead sleep of Midnight-Security hath surprised and overtaken them, that do not hear the loud Report of the many Divine Warning-Pieces that are gone off among us?"[233] says Increase Mather's friend, Urian Oakes, in the preface to Mather's published sermon, *The Day of Trouble is Near* (1674). Increase faced throughout his career the same terrible problem Edwards found critical—that of awakening a backsliding people from their stupor in a period of heightened extra-religious tension. In March 1677, in the midst of King Philip's War, Increase called renewal of the covenant "the great duty incumbent on decaying or distressed churches."[234] And he resorted to imprecation. "Men by nature are fallen into a *horrible pit* of Sin, Guilt, Misery, Death and Destruction," he declared in a sermon of the early 1670s that worked up to a climactic incantation of *"Repent or perish, Repent or perish."*[235] Around the same time, he asked: "Do you think that I love to scare you, with the dark visions of that Eternal Night which is hastening upon your Souls?"[236] He said he thought he was more in his element when speaking of God's pardoning grace, but that religious decay and indifference forced him to uncongenial excoriation.

The over-emphatic, whiplash style of Cotton Mather can be seen as a constant response to the same indifference. Cotton excoriated more mildly, in proportion as the period from 1700 to 1725 presented a milder face than the earthquake-scarred 17th century. Behind the outward composure of the early 18th century, as Cotton well knew, vaster changes than any that had yet wrenched America were in the making. Stoddard sensed something of the sort. He felt he had the best chance to reverse the creeping rigor mortis of Puritanism if he managed to bring entire communities under his authority by welcoming everyone into the church indiscriminately. Though the terrors of the people might seem great, "yet they need to be greater," said Stoddard: "if they be but thorowly scared, they will be brought to an universal Reformation . . . ."[237]

Edwards would never raise his voice or flail his arms while preaching; he, furthermore, fell into that group of the clergy known as *moderate* revivalists. An unequivocal supporter of the Great Awakening, he nevertheless pursued tactics that where thoroughgoing rather than violent or extreme. He took his listeners step by step over many weeks or months in a planned logical progression that solidly prepared them for a decisive moment of commitment. *God glorified in the Work of Redemption* of 8 July 1731 may be regarded as the opening gun of a systematic campaign of revival, as well as his first overt assault against Arminianism. By 1734 he had hit his matchless stride, with *A Divine and Supernatural Light; The Excellency of Christ;* possibly *The Christian Pilgrim* (whose date is not certainly known); a sequence on *Justification by Faith Alone;* and the climax of another sequence, *The Justice of God in the Damnation of Sinners.*

Revival passion flared spectacularly in the winter of 1735, as Edwards's relentless sequences of sermons showed no sign of slackening. It was the greatest, as it was the most carefully spaded, revival ever known anywhere in New England at any time in history, and it set off the universal Great Awakening. Late that spring of 1735, one Thomas Stebbins tried to commit suicide. Several weeks later, Edwards's uncle, Joseph Hawley, a leading citizen of Northampton, succeeded, by slitting his throat. Other suicides and attempted suicides followed. But there were 300 converts, and the new 56' x 70' meetinghouse was finished in September 1736.

Edwards kept pressing the attack, but in long, slow crescendos. In the summer of 1741 he reached a new high climax, Valley-wide, with *Sinners in the Hands of an Angry God,* which topped a building sequence that included *The Future Punishment of the Wicked Unavoidable and Intolerable* three weeks before. He read *Sinners in the Hands of an Angry God* July 8 nearby Enfield, Connecticut, in a quiet and deliberate manner (like Calvin or Shepard), but to a steady accompaniment of wailing from the audience, which grew hysterical.

DR. CHARLES CHAUNCY of Boston's First Church resisted the

rage of revivalism from the summer of 1742 as a dangerous new outbreak of Antinomian enthusiasm. He called it a disease, a sort of madness, caused by a bad temperament of the blood and spirits. Those most in danger of it, he said, were those in whom *melancholy* was the prevailing ingredient in their constitutions. Sometimes a certain wildness was descernible in their general look and air, as they mistook the workings of their own passions for divine communications.[238]

Edwards cringed at enthusiasm himself. He did not go so far as Chauncy—or John Wesley, who thought any such manifestation either gin or humbug. But religion, insisted Edwards, must affect the heart to be valid, and irregularities were to be expected in a time of great awakenings of the heart. He held true throughout, however, to quiet Augustinian contemplation as opposed to "enthusiasm":

For my part [he said in the post-commencement discourse at New Haven 10 September 1741 which won the graduating senior Hopkins as a disciple], I had rather enjoy the sweet Influences of the Spirit, shewing Christ's spiritual divine Beauty, and infinite Grace, and dying Love, drawing forth the holy Exercises of Faith, and divine Love, and sweet Complacence, and humble Joy in God, one Quarter of an Hour, than to have prophetical Visions and Revelations for a whole Year.

Under the spell of "enthusiasm," he continues, people are known to "leave the Guidance of the Pole Star, to follow *a Jack with a Lanthorn.*"

And seeing Inspiration is not to be expected, let us not despise human Learning. They say that human Learning is of little or no Use in the Work of the Ministry, don't consider what they say . . . .[239]

Compare Increase Mather:

But if every piece of Ignorance and Arrogance be set up for a *Preacher,* the Name of the Holy God will be prophaned with an *Offering* that is made a *Ridicule* in the *Repetition* . . . . *Though* some *Unlearned* Men have been useful to the Interests of *Religion,* yet no Man ever decried *Learning,* but what was an Enemy to *Religion* . . . .[240]

We nevertheless easily perceive that the learned Chauncy

was much closer to the modern temper than Increase or Edwards in wishing to suppress excess emotion in religion as a vulgar interference with rational concentration on the Bible.

Chauncy preached the funeral sermon for his intimate friend Jonathan Mayhew, the pastor of Boston's West Church who had scandalously turned Arminian. Chauncy's disposition also inclined him naturally to Arminianism, and in 1782 he finally published a book under the pseudonym-initials "T. W." entitled *Salvation for All Men, Illustrated and Vindicated as a Scripture Doctrine.*

Cotton Mather's son Samuel remained true to his father with a reply: *All Men Will Not Be Saved Forever.* And Edwards's son Jonathan Jr. remained true to his father with a fuller reply: *The Salvation of All Men Strictly Examined; and the Endless Punishment of Those who Die Impenitent, Argued and Defended against the Objections and Reasonings of the Late Rev. Doctor Chauncy.* "A mistake here may be fatal," the younger Edwards echoes the greatest of the anti-Arminians.[241]

To PERRY MILLER, Edwards's revival preaching "was America's sudden leap into modernity" because it brought his hearers without mitigation, protection, or indulgence face to face with a cosmos fundamentally inhuman.[242] Edwards did preach during Amercia's leap into modernity, but his preaching was not the leap. It was more the desperate effort to prevent the leap.

Edwards not only did not toss out the mitigating covenant in such preaching; the point of *Sinners in the Hands of an Angry God* is to awake men to take advantage of the covenant before it is too late. "The use of this awful subject may be for awakening unconverted persons in this congregation," Edwards says explicitly. "Haste and escape for your lives ... escape to the mountain [Zion, no doubt], lest you be consumed."

But it is only the "unconverted," those "not in Christ," the "unregenerate," the "wicked" that Edwards says are condemned. *"There is nothing that keeps wicked men, at any one moment, out of hell, but the meer pleasure of GOD."* Just *"wicked men."* God, Edwards continues, is "under no manner of obligation" to keep "any natural man" who "does not believe in any of the promises" of the covenant or who has no "interest in the mediator of the covenant" "a *moment* from eternal destruction." "Thus are all you that never passed under a great change of heart," i.e. "were never born again . . . ."

Sincere converts are excepted. It is only the wicked who "have no refuge, nothing to take hold of." And it is the "arbitrary will, and uncovenanted . . . . forbearance" of God, only, that preserves the wicked who have not yet gone to perdition.[243]

THE INCIPIENT ARMINIANISM in this preaching—man can save himself by accepting the covenant of his own free will—might deceive us into missing the crux of the controversy. For here again Edwards was the culminator of a long tradition rather than the innovator of a new one.

In the middle of the 17th century, the distinguished first-generation minister of Roxbury, John Eliot, was telling the Massachusetts Indians that "Every man that truely believeth in Jesus Christ shall goe to heaven."[244] When Increase Mather repeated *"Repent or perish,"* he was implicitly saying that if you *do* repent, an angry God is under contract to save you from perishing in the hot, black pit. The very title of his imprecatory sermon has an Arminian ring: *Christians ought to work out their own Salvation.* In 1716 he preached on the explicit doctrine *"That God will graciously hear and answer the Prayers of the Righteous."*[245] When Cotton Mather warned in 1712 to make due provision "That when you *Dy,* you may *Sleep Comfortably,"* his controlling assumption is that you can do something about the restfulness of your sleep after death. This hopeful element lies equally basic in the scare-warnings of Edwards, who assumes that waking up to the reality of the danger is tantamount to escaping it. What worries him, as the Mathers, is not that nothing can be done about it, but that people miss the necessity of doing something.

Young Whitefield illustrates the same essential paradox of "Arminian" Calvinism in his altercation yith John Wesley. Wesley takes the frankly-Arminian position that predestination "tends to destroy the Comforts of Religion." He says it also "tends to destroy Holiness, by wholly taking away the first Motives to follow after it, *viz.* the Hope of Heaven and the Fear of Hell." Whitefield answers in surprise: "to hear the Whispers of the Enemy [Arminius], reviving from the Mouth, and Pen, of the Reverend and learned Mr. *Wesley,* gives me Rood to apprehend, That there is none, in Time, can plead Exemption from sinning."[246]

Yet Whitefield's tremendous appeal in America lay largely

in his convincing people they all could and should save themselves. Consider his classic *"morning* glory" of Wednesday 8 October 1741, which left few dry eyes among his audience and caused the greatest commotion he achieved in Boston. This occurred in Webb's New North meetinghouse, to which Whitefield rode with the governor in the royal coach.

A little before I had heard of a Child [Whitefield recounts], who was taken sick just after it had heard me preach, and said, 'He would go to Mr. *Whitefield's* God,' and died in a short Time. This encouraged me to speak to little Ones. But, oh how were the old People affected, when I said, 'Little Children, if your Parents will not come to Christ, do you come and go to Heaven without them.' [247]

So the Calvinist who twitted Wesley on his Arminianism ("Free Grace Indeed!") was even calling on little children to save themselves!

Edwards set about systematically answering Arminianism in his monumental monograph on *Freedom of Will.* He vigorously propounds that *"the Will is always determined by the strongest Motive,* or by that View of the Mind which has the greatest Degree of *previous* Tendency to excite Volition," and twenty pages later he puts the triumphant question "whether it be not plainly absurd, and a manifest Inconsistence, to suppose that *the Will itself determines all the free Acts of the Will."*[248] But after defending predestination along this line, he shifts to that Calvinist position continued in the tradition of Hobbes, Milton, Locke, and Hume whereby, after bewilderingly entangling himself, Edwards winds up contending that man has sufficient free choice to be held responsible for his acts and to take the consequences. It is not such an entanglement if Richard P. Cecil is right in suggesting that Edwards defends free will in the deterministic tradition of Spinoza, Hegel, and Marx that freedom is the recognition of necessity.

Edwards had put the Calvinist case according to an alternative position of Calvin's (for the basic contradiction is present in Calvin—or in reality) in his *Treatise on Grace,* wherein he concludes that though knowledge, reform, and conviction preparatory to conversion may come gradually, conversion itself is wrought at once, by God.

Hence we may learn that *it is impossible for men to convert themselves* by their own strength and industry . . . . All that men can do by their own strength and industry is only gradually to increase and improve and new-model and direct qualities, principles, and perfections of nature that they have already.[249]

Yet Edwards also (orthodoxly) says at another time that *"Perseverence in faith, is, in one sense, the condition of justification; that is, the promise of acceptance is made only to a persevering sort of faith; and the proper evidence of its being of that sort, is actual perseverance."* Perseverance in faith will give more of a disposition and resolution to persevere and more of a spirit of dependence on God and Christ to enable perseverance.[250]

This greater and greater spirit of dependence on the divine brings with it, in Edwards's thinking, a sense of the sweetness of God's absolute sovereignty. And this sense in turn underlies Edwards's famous definition of virtue:

True virtue most essentially consists in benevolence to Being [i.e. love of God] in general. Or perhaps to speak more accurately, it is that consent, propensity and union of heart to Being in general, that is immediately exercised in a general good-will . . . . Yea, spiritual beauty consists wholly in this, and the various qualities and exercises of mind which proceed from it, and the external actions which proceed from these internal qualities and exercises.[251]

By this avenue or others Edwards always returns to the love of God, and for him this always carries the corollary of emotional involvement. "The Author of the human Nature" had made emotions (affections) "very much the Spring of Men's Actions." Not only religion but life itself is largely an emotional matter. "Take away all *Love* and *Hatred*, all *Hope* and *Fear*, all *Anger*, *Zeal*, and affectionate *Desire*, and the world would be, in great Measure, motionless and dead . . . ."[252]

In the light of this constant theme, it becomes unmistakably clear, regardless of the gallant smoke-screen of *Freedom of Will*, that what Arminianism essentially signified to Edwards was *halfheartedness* or *lukewarmness*, a substitution of moralism and respectability for a deeply-felt allegiance of the spirit.

THE REVIVAL DIED in Northampton in the year 1744, merely a few months after Edwards's expansive statement late in 1743 that it might be the beginning of a worldwide renewal of mankind.

In March 1744 the church denied Edwards's request for a fixed salary, and this indicates a turn of some degree against him—certainly a loss of awe and likely a depletion of revival enthusiasm. "Depletion" might even be an understatement; for nearly every New England community experienced a post-revival letdown and revulsion such as tends to follow any form of protracted intoxication.

In that same March 1744 the "bad book" case broke. Some of the youth were reported using what was regarded as lascivious or obscene language picked up from a certain book or books, probably a manual for midwives, in the possession of friends. Edwards proceeded to handle the complaint by publicly reading the names of the boys and girls he required to appear for interrogation; but he did not discriminate between known hoodlums and children of "considerable" families when he read the list. He also departed from the "church-way" tradition in that he broached a disciplinary matter publicly before dealing with it first privately.

Commentators ever since have been sure that he committed a major tactical error. But it is at least as probable that Edwards, consciously or unconsciously, had opened his retaliatory attack upon a congregation, especially certain considerable families in it, that had betrayed the Lord by their relaxation of religious constancy, and had (as a consequence of this) denied Edwards just compensation and gone on to criticize his standard of living and his saintly wife's fashionable apparel. That very spring of 1744, says Hopkins, was the time that Edwards first divulged his new covenant strictures.

No candidates for membership presented themselves for four years—another certain sign of the death of the revival; so Edwards had to postpone invoking his redefined covenant doctrine until 1748, when a candidate appeared and opened the fatal showdown.

Meanwhile, Edwards's "bad book" investigation ground on as though to freeze the town in its disdain. The adolescents summoned for questioning took the whole matter as a lark, but Edwards finally got confessions from the three unsavory ringleaders, and closed the affair 3 June 1744 by publicly reading their statements. It was a Pyrrhic victory; for Edwards's handling of this affair, which from the first had had

Northampton "all on a Blaze," as Hopkins puts it, is what weakened his influence with many heads of families and especially the young folk, says Hopkins.

All this time, too, Edwards pressed his battle for a fixed salary. The cooled-off congregation probably thought they had been amply generous by their salary raises of 1740 and '41. But in 1747, finally, he won this point as well. It amounted to another Pyrrhic victory, because the long dispute consolidated the opposition that lay ready to ambush his covenant demands. Many months before the 16 May 1748 formal signing of the salary agreement, Edwards, who already had three servants for his large and growing household, poured fresh fuel on the flames of public opinion by buying a Negro slave girl (named Venus). Whatever the extent that this and the fact that he got his expensive clothes tailored in Boston, antagonized his fellow hinterlanders, their sullen resentment of pastoral privilege and prerogative turned out to be the beginning of a widening movement throughout New England to curtail the clergy's traditional elevation over their congregations.[253]

So the revival had been dead four years when Edwards calmly walked through the ruins of his fondest hopes and engaged his congregation in a mortal struggle to determine whether he or anemic Arminianism would prevail in the Northampton church. His chief prosecutor turned out to be the 26-year-old lawyer-son of that uncle of Edwards who committed suicide in 1735. Edwards fought to the bitter end and never lost his composure; but the issue could hardly have been in doubt. "As to the state of religion in these parts of the world," he wrote a friend in Scotland 23 May 1749, "it is in the general very dark and melancholy." "Iniquity abounds, and the love of many waxes cold," he wrote another Scot 2 April 1750; "Arminianism, and Pelagianism, have made a strange progress within a few years."[254] If he could say in 1743 that what his congregation needed was to have their hearts touched, he had to admit by 1750 that their hearts were out of reach.

Here is the shortest of four forms of the covenant acceptable to Edwards:

I hope, I do truly find a heart to give up myself to God, according to the tenor of that covenant of grace which was sealed in my baptism, and to walk in a way of that obedience to all the commandments of God, so long as I live.[255]

He only required a *hope,* a sincere hope. This sounds so reasonable that, in spite of all the complicating additional issues involved, one can hardly help feeling that the congregation's resistance to pledging the covenant marks the final break, not merely with Edwards but with the whole 300-year Dissenter tradition of a purified church. Their unwillingness any longer to give more than lip-service to that ideal marks the decisive change of destination of the American pilgrimage.

LAVENGOOD shows in his new approach to the Great Awakening that of thirteen known cases of ministers dismissed from their pulpits in Massachusetts or Connecticut because of controversies growing out of the revival, eight were supporters of the revival. Of these eight, six were unrepentant young radicals and the other two the moderates Edwards and his friend Jonathan Billing of nearby Cold Spring (later Belchertown). Edwards and Billing both advocated, out of season, a repeal of Stoddardism and a return to the old Dissenter ideal of a purified church.[256]

By encouraging the revival, which inadvertently gave impetus to revolutionary forces dammed up awaiting some such opportunity to pour forth, preachers seemed to help revive themselves right out of their own pulpits. A rare example of a preacher who lost his pulpit because of being more conservative than his congregation was none other than Cotton Mather's son Samuel in Boston who minimized the revival as so much hysteria or, to use his tern, "enthusiasm." We have seen, however, that he too breasted the Arminian tide in support of the old Puritanism.

Edwards early and correctly gauged the threat of Arminianism. It was in the times, not just in the London tracts he refuted in *Freedom of Will* or in the isolated open avowal of Arminianism by the pastor of Boston's West Church in this period. "The Modern Prevailing Notions," Edwards calls Arminianism in the full title of *Freedom of Will.* He said it was about the fall of 1734 that "the great *Noise*" began in the Connecticut Valley concerning Arminianism, "which seemed to appear with a very *threatening* Aspect upon the Interest of Religion here"; but Cotton Mather had sounded the alarm against Arminianism as an adjunct of self-will and lethargy as early as 1692.[257] It is no mere coincidence that Edwards's Harvard-trained river-god relatives who pushed his ouster were Arminian. (Harvard had long had Arminian tendencies, while Edwards's alma mater, Yale, prided itself on remaining a bastion of true Puritanism.) Edwards's cousin, Israel Williams, the "monarch of Hampshire," in particular opposed Edwards's use of the pulpit for an open counter-attack on Arminianism. Edwards's defiance essentially generated the revival heat while making inveterate enemies of the Williams clan at the outset.

"Am I therefore become your Enemy, because I tell you the Truth?" Edwards quotes *Galatians* on the title page of his published farewell sermon. But by then, the Truth he held was no longer quite what his congregation took to be truth. By then they had switched to the Williams leadership. When Edwards warned them in his farewell sermon that they could expect to meet him again on the day of judgment,[258] they seemed more than willing to take their chances. Back in 1741 he had sobbed throughout the morning worship service that the 26-year-old Whitefield conducted at Northampton October 10. Edwards's congregation wept with him then, and also the day before.[259] He did not strike them in those times as forbiddingly cold. But as the years passed, he lost the touch with them that he had in eminent degree in the 1730s. The age of Franklin, now commencing, had made him, in hardly a decade, a stranger in his own land.

The fact that the Arminian river gods, i.e. the aristocratic political bosses of the Connecticut Valley, turned against Edwards does not at all mean that Edwards is to be identified with democratic forces arrayed against despotism. *Both* parties (the landed and the land-cramped) turned against Edwards, who lost his pulpit by an overwhelming vote of nearly ten to one. Robert Taylor's important study of western Massachusetts demonstrates that, after all, the "laggard" Valley remained politically conservative right up to the Revolution.[260] If Edwards were to be identified with any social or political group, it would have been the river gods.

He was related to every one of them. He wore a wig, also a white shirt when almost all the men in Northampton wore blue-checked shirts to church. He was not only the grandson, colleague, and successor of Solomon Stoddard, who ruled the Valley churches, but the nephew of the most powerful and inflexible magistrate of the Valley, Colonel John Stoddard, who was always protective of his young pastor-relative Jonathan. Not until Colonel Stoddard died in 1748 and Edwards had commemorated the passing of an era in the "withering" of this "*strong Rod*,"[261] did the other river gods rise to hasten the passing of Edwards with the era.

Edwards seems actually to have paid little attention to politics, which was irrelevant to the main questions in his mind. He always conformed to the political realities and *status quo* of his time and place, even to urging vigorous prosecution of war against the French and Indians in the summer of 1744. Political defection was not involved in his branding the Arminians of his office-holding relatives or in departing from his grandfather's conception of Communion. He was the least political of all the famous Puritans—and that could have been a large part of his trouble, as well as a sign of the end of the pilgrim era.

Edwards seemed to divine, in his fight for the primitive-church ideal and in his fight against Arminianism or lukewarmness, that he faced nothing less than this passing of the old order. It is significant that his emotions shortly before he entered upon his ministry in Northampton should at last have resembled those of the first generation of Puritans. The fact that the children and grandchildren of the founding Puritans could not bring about an inner agonizing conversion—or, evidently, to care whether they did or not—suggests that external crisis was what was lacking. Edwards, who worked so long in vain toward an authentic old-fashioned conversion, felt that very lack in himself and his time as a crisis.

The return, however, of a species of external crisis—caused by the great subsurface changes in American life—caught him in mid-career and reawakened, for a season, something of the emotional anguish and exaltation that the fathers had known. The continuity of context (or inertia of the tradition) remained so strong in New England between Edwards's generation and the generation of Eleazar and Increase Mather that the Dissenting synthesis persisted in America, at least in the back country, far beyond the late-17-century doldrums; whereas in these doldrums the tradition came to a virtual end in England.

In those late-17th-century doldrums in America, the Congregationalists still clung to the crisis-born Puritan Dissent with little change in form; but it no longer quite fit its setting. As the minister of Stamford, Connecticut put it, "Many are gospel-glutted, & growing weary."[262] He was referring to aged communicants but all too accurately described the younger-aged as well. We have seen Cotton Mather at the turn of the century sobered by the *Dying Times*. His one-time tutor, Peter Thatcher, long since pastor at Milton, preached and published his most notable sermon in 1708: *Unbelief Detected and Condemned*. The dragginess to which church singing had everywhere degenerated a decade or two before this, mirrored the pervasive loss of interest in religious habits of the past.[263] "There is now a great Decay amongst Professors of Religion in this Land," Increase Mather lamented in November 1699 in his preface to Samuel Willard's *The Peril of the Times Displayed*.[264] This had already become an almost ritualistic dirge; the day had for some time arrived when Puritanism wailingly preoccupied itself with its own passing. The "peril of the times" that distressed the distinguished Boston clergyman Willard and all his colleagues was the loss of the spirit of godliness while retaining merely its form—what Edwards would call Arminianism.

But their unremitting efforts to revive a people they kept assailing as in "declension" did, in the last analysis, help preserve the old modes of mind and bore sporadic fruit in local revivals throughout New England almost from the opening of the 18th century. When a revival became universal in 1740-41, it did give the old Puritan orthodoxy a new lease on life and entrenched it more deeply in the small towns of the hinterland. "Great Awakening" is, after all, the clergy's interpretation of the movement; Edwards had used the term "Great Awakenings" in the subtitle of his *Sinners in the Hands of an Angry God* while the revival was in process.

The religious revival, however, stimulated bumptious secular and levelling tendencies already adolescent. Back at the turn of the century Willard had perceived not merely weariness with the old but a threatening eagerness for the new:

many grow *weary of Christ's yoke,* and seek for more *liberty* . . . . how doth vanity, and a fondness after new things abound among them? how do young persons grow weary of the strict profession of their fathers, and become strong disputants for those things which their Progenitors forsook a pleasant Land for the avoidance of . . .? Besides, it is almost a general complaint of Family Governours, that their Children and Servants are weary of the yoke, and are not willing to be under their Command . . . . the life of Religion is panting and gasping among us . . . . There is an unhappy Generation of men in the world, who would fain perswade

others to think that they have arrived at higher degrees of per-
tion than their neighbours . . . .[265]

The roused emotions of the religious revival unexpectedly unleashed these long-present new tendencies or, to continue in
Willard's imagery, broke the yoke.

SINCE THIS REVOLUTION to modernity, which the Great Awakening represents as well as a revival of waning Puritanism,
Americans—along with the rest of the west—have increasingly
suspected that "everlasting Life" was everlasting death; and
death has been the subject to be most avoided of most considered. They have increasingly refused to "take order" from
Scripture or to grant the Bible a greater validity than experience or nature.[266] Like that anti-Platonist Jefferson, they
have turned ever more frankly Epicurean, believing in no
afterlife but a dissolution and recombination of matter. The
question Edwards propounded, opening "If there be really a
Hell," would have met more and more with a mere smile.

Edwards himself, meanwhile, could not entirely escape the
Jefferson-and-Franklin-type attachment to the world, which
he said the pilgrim should grimly endure while trudging uphill
through. Even when Edwards is truest to otherworldly Plato-
nism, he is most freshly aware of the tangible beauty of his
analogy:

the Son of God created the world . . . to communicate Himself
in an image of His own excellency. He communicates Himself,
properly, only to spirits, and they only are capable of being
proper images of His excellency, for they only are properly
beings . . . . Yet he communicates a sort of shadow, or glimpse,
of His excellencies to bodies, which . . . are but shadows of
beings, and not real beings . . . . the beauties of nature are really
the emanations or shadows of the excellencies of the Son of God
. . . . That beauteous light with which the world is filled in a
clear day, is a lively shadow of His spotless holiness, and a happiness and delight in communicating Himself . . . . But we see far
the most proper image of the beauty of Christ when we see beauty
in the human soul.[267]

Are the shadows a sufficient inducement to the pilgrim to put
his burden down and linger in the strange wilderness? "How
lovely is the green of the face of the earth in all manner of

colours, in flowers, the colour of the skies, and lovely tinctures of the morning and evening," Edwards pauses in his own pilgrimage to gaze about. "Hence the reason why almost all men, and those that seem to be very miserable, love life, because they cannot bear to lose sight of such a beautiful and lovely world."[268]

Epilogue:

Lincoln's Voyage

O memory! thou mid-way world
'Twixt Earth and Paradise,
Where things decayed, and loved ones lost
In dreamy shadows rise . . . .
Till every sound appears a knell,
And every spot a grave.
—ABRAHAM LINCOLN, *My Childhood-Home*
I See Again, 1846

WHILE such an anti-Platonist child of the Enlightenment as Jefferson was serious to the point of humorlessness but with a sunny countenance, Lincoln in the century of romantic reaction was incessantly joking but sad of visage. Those who laughed loud at Lincoln's jokes tended to remember him as "kind" and "sad," as though they perceived that the joking was not the key to the man who easily wept. Those who were most intimate—and he showed an easy familiarity to everybody—called him "Mr. Lincoln" because of a certain distance and reserve that barred real closeness except superficially. One suspects that the jokes served the function of making close contact with others and of keeping them at arm's length simultaneously, and of a safety-valve reaction to inner preoccupations of another nature.

He had periods of melancholy bordering on psychosis. We know little about them and can scarcely evaluate their significance; that includes the significance of the debilitating attacks of depression he suffered as a young legislator at Vandalia in 1836. One of his fellow legislators later told Willam Herndon that Lincoln said his mental depression became so intense at times that he never dared carry a pocket knife. "His melancholy dripped from him as he walked," says Herndon, Lincoln's law partner, who also points out that Lincoln's mother, Nancy Hanks, had "a marked expression of melancholy which fixed itself in the memory of everyone who ever knew her." Herndon felt certain that Lincoln's "morbid condition" was hereditary, also occult. "It was ingrained . . . . it was part of his nature, and could no more be shaken off then he could part with his brains."[269] His features were graven with sorrow. Henry Adams refers to that "plain, ploughed face." Another observer, Horace White, recalls "a shade of melancholy drawn like a veil over his whole face."

In repose, his face was dull, lifeless, repellent, viewers agreed. He often seemed to withdraw from the world and to be unaware of what was going on about him. Herndon speaks of his being frequently in "deep abstraction." Some acquaintances concluded him to be essentially cold and aloof. The characteristic sadness as well as the remoteness is most notable in his last heartbreaking photograph, in which he appears completely in another world, an unseeing distant look in his eyes and a faint, sad smile on his face.

Behind those sad and dreamy and often unseeing gray eyes, another life went on with great intensity. We know little about it because he kept it to himself. His grief-stricken face, his fits of melancholia, his lone walks at midnight, the complex allusiveness of his deceptively-crystalline prose, his rare references to his fatalism, his heavy-silence reaction to the death of his son Willie in the White House, to his wife's progressive insanity, to his more-and-more urgent awareness of the sickeningness of slavery, and to the staggering horror of the war, and his September 1862 memorandum that opens "The will of God prevails," all give oblique evidence of this other life. Was his inward concentration directed to a solitary mystic journey?

His preoccupation (obsession?) with death apparently began before he left for Washington. He told Herndon that the feeling had become irrepressible that he would never return to Springfield alive. When Herndon replied that such a notion was not in keeping with the popular ideal of a President, Lincoln quickly retorted "But it is in keeping with my philosophy."[270] One wonders how much of his consciousness may have been taken up with thoughts of death, especially when Melville, Hawthorne, Whitman, and surprisingly even Mark Twain, devoted their writing during the same time so extensively to death. Lincoln, who never outgrew his superstitious Kentucky childhood, including a belief in dreams as portents, dreamed in the White House long before his assassination that he went downstairs and heard sounds of sobbing over somebody's death. Looking in the coffin, he discovered the corpse to be himself.

He had a recurrent dream (recurrence is significant), often, he said, before military disasters or decisive victories,

a dream of floating—floating away on some vast and indistinct expanse, toward an unknown shore,

as Frederick Seward reported Lincoln's words 14 April 1865.[271]

A death wish in the sense of a desire for extinction would seem entirely out of keeping with Lincoln's complicated, enigmatic, but affirmative character, though his character seemed immersed in deep weariness. He brushed aside any apparent longing for physical rest; "the tired part of me," he said in 1862, "is *inside* and out of reach." Evidently he *did* long for rest of that. Kenneth Burke, taking his cue from C. G. Jung, shows the so-called death wish of modern literature to be an incomplete part of a death-and-*rebirth pattern*. A death wish in the sense of a desire to ascend to the City of Rest and everlasting "Life" would be a conjecture with at least some plausibility for Lincoln.

If the vast and indistinct expanse were the calm River Jordan, and the unknown shore the other world, Lincoln was, perhaps subconsciously, a pilgrim.

THE PSYCHOANALYTICAL SYMBOL of the sea as the unconscious and also as a desire to return to the womb agrees with the Christian pilgrim's desire to return home to the Author of his being. Emily Dickinson, who wrote her poems in Lincoln's century and who frequently alluded to her own pilgrimage sometimes with the very word "pilgrim," said in 1863: "I can-

not tell how Eternity seems. It sweeps around me like a sea."
One of her poems bears the title *On this wondrous sea*, and another has the lines

> *'Tis little I could care for pearls*
> *Who own the ample sea* . . . .

the "ample sea" being immortality. She is speaking as one
dying, who in death will be crowned queen. In still another
poem she refers to the pilgrimage this way:

> *Our journey had advanced* . . . .
> *Retreat was out of hope,—*
> *Behind, a sealed route,*
> *Eternity's white flag before*
> *And God at every gate.*[272]

A closer contemporary of Lincoln, the Quaker poet John
Greenleaf Whittier, alludes to the imminent end of his pilgrimage in *The Eternal Goodness*:

> *And so beside the Silent Sea*
> *I wait the muffled oar* . . . .

A popular hymn of the period, the words by a John Ellerton,
goes in part:

> *Now upon the farther shore*
> *Lands the voyager at last* . . . .

Tennyson, too, would almost seem to be interpreting Lincoln's
dream:

> *. . . May there be no moaning of the bar,*
> *When I put out to sea* . . .
> *When that which drew from out the boundless deep*
> *Turns again home.*
>
> *Twilight and evening bell,*
> *And after that the dark!*
>
> *And may there be no sadness of farewell,*
> *When I embark;*

> *. . . I hope to see my Pilot face to face*
> *When I have crossed the bar.*

D. H. Lawrence extends the metaphor of the sea:

> *Build then the ship of death, for you must take*
> *the longest journey, to oblivion . . .*
> *Already the dark and endless ocean of the end*
> *is washing in . . . .*
>
> *But dipped, once dipped in dark oblivion*
> *the soul has peace, inward and lovely peace.*[273]

When Faust contemplates suicide in Goethe's early 19th century poem, he does so in terms of the beckoning open sea, of another day on a new shore, and of a chariot swinging to meet him.

Thomas Hooker in the early 17th century used the image of a boat in speaking of the mystic crossing from mundane anxiety to divine peace. Before going to sleep (which the Puritans often used as a metaphor for death), Hooker would ponder some promise of God's in the Bible until it gave him sufficient assurance to relax in sleep. "The promise," he would counsel others, "was the boat, which was to carry a perishing sinner over into the Lord Jesus Christ."[274] We are "but passengers in a Ship," Roger Williams said. (Buddhism stresses the metaphor of a raft.) "You know how Eternity hangs upon a moment," wrote Hugh Peter to his daughter. "It is a vast Ocean, hath neither bound nor bottom . . . ."[275] The poetminister of Cambridge, John Adams, composed a poem on the death of two boys who fell through the ice in January 1728:

> *And now, forever, ever drown'd,*
> *Sink in a Sea without a Bound*
> *O happy! rescu'd from the Cares,*
> *The numerous Woes and horrid Fears,*
> *Which spread this ever-gloomy Scene,*
> *This Pilgrims ill-attended Inn.*[276]

AT THE CLOSE of the second part of *Pilgrim's Progress*, a work Lincoln grew up on, Christian's wife Christina receives the call of the Master and enters the River Jordan. On the other side are horses and chariots waiting to accompany her up Mount Zion to the city gate. Then at the very end of the book, Mr. Stand-fast goes down to the river, which is in a time of great calm. While he is discoursing when half-way in, his countenance changes and he ceases to be seen.

The open region fills with horses and chariots, trumpeters and pipers, singers, and players on stringed instruments, to welcome the pilgrims as they go up and follow one another in "at the beautiful Gate of the City."

Notes

[1]*The Heavenly City of the Eighteenth-Century Philosophers* (New Haven: Yale 1932), p. 31

[2]*A Faithful Narrative of the Surprizing Work of God in the Conversion of Many Hundred Souls in Northampton, and the Neighbouring Towns and Villages of New-Hampshire in New England. In a Letter to the Revd. Dr. Benjamin Colman of Boston . . . Nov. 6 1736* (London 1737), p. 32

[3]Albert Matthews, "The Term Pilgrim Fathers and Early Celebrations of Fore-fathers' Day," Col. Soc. Mass. *Pubs.*, XVII, 355. The Greek word translated "pilgrims" was (transliterated) *parepidemoi.*

[4]*Of Plimmoth Plantation,* fac. edition (London 1896), p. 91

[5]Nathaniel Morton, *New England's Memorial,* 5th edition, ed. John Davis (Boston 1826), p. 264

[6]*Returning unto God the Great Concernment of a Covenant People* (Boston 1680), p. 1

[7]Jonathan Edwards, *The Christian Pilgrim, or The Christian Life a Journey towards Heaven,* in *Works,* ed. Sereno Dwight (N.Y. 1830), VII, 137, 140-41

[8]Quotations from *Phaedo* are in the Benjamin Jowett translation, numerous editions; from the *Republic,* the translation of Francis MacDonald Cornford (N.Y. & London: Oxford U. 1945). Many editions of *Pilgrim's Progress,* old and new, have been used; principally: John Bunyan. *The Pilgrim's Progress from this World, to that which is to come: delivered under the Similitude of a Dream* [Part I] (London 1678), fac. edition (London: Noel Douglas Replicas 1928) and both Parts, ed. J. B. Warey (Oxford: Clarendon Press 1928). Part II was first published in 1685. The two Parts went into innumerable editions both separately and combined.

[9]First Ennead, 3. 3; Fifth Ennead, 9. 1, *The Six Enneads,* tr. Stephen MacKenna and B. S. Page, *Great Books of the Western World,* ed. Robert Maynard Hutchins (Chicago, London, Toronto: Encyclopedia Britannica 1952), XVII, 10-11, 246

[10]Cuthbert Butler, *Western Mysticism: the Teaching of SS. Augustine, Gregory and Bernard on Contemplation and the Contemplative Life,* 2nd edition (London: Dutton 1926; reprint 1951), pp. 157, 158, 163

[11]*On Christian Doctrine,* tr. J. F. Shaw [T & T Clark, Edinburgh], *Great Books,* XVIII, 625, 627, 628, 629, 632, 639

[12]*The City of God,* tr. Marcus Dods [T & T Clark, Edinburgh], *ibid.,* 401, 421, 464, 503, 507, 520, 522-23

[13]See particularly Perry Miller, *The New England Mind: the Seventeenth Century* (Cambridge: Harvard U. 1939), chap. 1: "The Augustinian Strain of Piety," pp. 4-10

[14]*Institutes of the Christian Religion*, Bk. IV, chap. 20, par. 2

[15]"The Catechism of the Church of Geneva that is a Plan for Instructing Children in the Doctrine of Christ," *Theological Treatises*, tr. J.K.S. Reid (London: SCM 1954), p. 104

[16]*A Selection of the Most Celebrated Sermons of John Calvin* (Philadelphia 1860), pp. 69-70

[17]Quoted in William Haller, *The Rise of Puritanism* (N.Y.: Columbia U. 1938), p. 149

[18]R. C. Winthrop, *Life and Letters of John Winthrop*, 2nd edition, 2 vols. (Boston 1869), I, 129-30, 290

[19]*The Winthrop Papers*, 5 vols. (Boston: MHS 1929-47), II, 151

[20]*A Short Story of the Rise, Reign, and Ruine of the Antinomians* (London 1644), preface

[21]Charles Eliot Norton, ed., *The Poems of Mrs. Anne Bradstreet* (n.p. 1897), p. 262; A. B., *Meditations Divine and Morall* (msc. in Houghton Library), p. 98

[22]*George Fox Digg'd out of his Burrovves* (Boston 1676), Narr. Club *Pubs.*, V (Providence 1872), p. 276

[23]*Harris Papers*, ed. Clarence S. Brigham, RIHS *Colls.*, X (1902), p. 150

[24]*The Mystery of Christ Opened and Applyed* (Boston 1686) p. 2

[25]*A Sermon concerning Obedience & Resignation to the Will of God* (Boston 1714), p. 38

[26]"An Attestation," in Cotton Mather, *Coelestinus* (Boston 1723), p. i (D3)

[27]*Meditations on Death and on the Believers Deliverance from the Fear of it* (Boston 1717), p. 111

[28]*Coelestinus*, p. 45

[29]*Paterna* (msc. in Alderman Library), p. 2. He also calls it "my *private* Walk," p. 111.

[30]*Coheleth* (Boston 1720), pp. 1-2

[31]*Agricola* (Boston 1727), p. 21

[32]*The Faithful Ministers of Christ Mindful of their own Death* (Boston 1729), p. 24

[33]*Familiar Letters to a Gentleman, upon a Variety of Seasonable and Important Subjects in Religion* (Boston 1745), Letter 19: "Containing particular Advices and Directions, for a close and comfortable *Walk with God*," pp. 402-24

[34]*Poems on Several Occasions* (Boston 1745), p. 19

[35]"Fragments from the Lost Writings of Irenaeus," *The Ante-Nicene Fathers*, ed. Alexander Roberts, James Donaldson, and A. Cleveland Coxe (Buffalo 1887), I, 570

[36]Epistle X, in *Select Letters*, tr. J. H. Baxter (London: Heinemann; N.Y.: Putnam's 1930), p. 11

[37]*Manuductio ad Ministerium. Directions for a Candidate of the Ministry* (Boston 1726), pp. 1-2

[38]*Death Made Easie & Happy* (London 1701), pp. 28-29, 50

[39]*Ibid.*, 1-3, 23

[40]*Ibid.*, 55, 94, 105

[41]*Ibid.*, 94

[42]*The Comfortable Chambers Opened and Visited* (Boston 1796), p. 12. See Augustine, *The Soliloquies*, tr. Thomas F. Gilligan (N.Y.: Cosmopolitan Science & Art 1943), Bk. II, chap. 13, "Of the Proof of the Soul's Immortality," pp. 121-23

[43]*Awakening Thoughts on the Sleep of Death* (Boston 1712), pp. 5, 29. *Cf.* Martin Luther, preface to *Spiritual Hymns Newly Revised at Wittenberg* (1529), *Works* (Philadelphia: Holman 1932), II, 228

[44]*The Comfortable Chambers*, pp. 11-12

[45]*A Good Man Making a Good End* (Boston 1698), pp. 17, 27. *Cf.* Increase Mather, *The Glorious Throne* (Boston 1702)

[46]*A Farewel Exhortation to the Church and People of Dorchester in New-England* (Cambridge 1657), p. 26

[47]*Works*, ed. Robert Ashton (Boston 1851), I, 257, 259

[48]*The Death of a Prophet Lamented and Improved* (Boston 1729), pp. 12-13

[49]*The Fatihful Ministers of Christ*, pp. 23-25

[50][Samuel Hopkins,] *The Life and Character of the Late Reverend Mr. Jonathan Edwards* (Boston 1765), p. 19; 3 Feb. 1725

[51]*Ibid.*, p. 6

[52][S. E. Dwight,] *The Life of President Edwards* (N.Y. 1830), p. 69

[53]*The Christian Pilgrim*, p. 138

[54]*Experiments of Spiritual Life & Health, and their Preservatives* (London 1652; reprint

Providence 1863), pp. 1, 57-59

[55]Letter (6 May 1682), 2 Mass. Hist. Soc. *Colls.*, VIII, 198

[56]*Letters and Papers of Roger Williams*, comp. Howard M. Chapin (Boston: MHS 1924), unnumbered photostat

[57]*Coheleth*, p. 7

[58]*A Comment upon Christ's Last Prayer in the Seventeenth of John. Wherein is opened, the Union Beleevers have with God and Christ* (London 1656), p. 110

[59]*Three Valuable Pieces . . . and a Private Diary; containing Meditations and Experiences never before published* (Boston 1747), "Meditations and Spiritual Experiences," p. 27

[60]Fifth Ennead, 9. 1-2; Sixth Ennead, 9. 11, pp. 246, 360

[61]*On Christian Doctrine*, I. 11, 17, pp. 627, 628

[62]Butler, *Western Mysticism*. p. 23. Other quotations from Augustine, if not specifically noted, are either in Butler's translation or E. B. Pusey's of the *Confessions*, the latter in various editions, mainly Everyman's Library. See also Willard L. Sperry, *Strangers & Pilgrims; Studies in Classics of Christian Devotion* (Boston: Little, Brown 1939), and Stringfellow Barr, *The Pilgrimage of Western Man* (N.Y.: Harcourt, Brace 1949).

[63]Hopkins, *Life of Edwards*, p. 26

[64]Clarence H. Faust and Thomas H. Johnson, eds., *Jonathan Edwards: Representative Selections* (N.Y.: American 1939), pp. 60, 63, 69

[65]*Winthrop Papers*, I, 156, 159

[66]*Mr. Cottons Letter Lately Printed, Examined and Ansvvered* (London 1644), p. 16

[67]"Meditation and Spiritual Experiences," p. 3

[68]*Select Letters*, p. 11

[69]Butler, *Western Mysticism*, p. 50

[70]*A Demonstration of True Love unto You the Rulers of the Colony of Massachusetts* (London 1674), p. 20

[71]See John Whiting, *Truth and Innocency Defended* (London 1702), p. 103; George Bishope, *New England Judged*, Part II (London 1667), p. 69; Mather, *Magnalia Christi Americana* (London 1702), Bk. VII, chap. IV, pp. 21-25; Thomas Chalkley, *Journal and Christian Experiences*, quoted in George Francis Dow, ed., *Two Centuries of Travel in Essex County . . . . 1605-1799* (Topsfield, Mass.: Topsfield HS 1921), p. xiv; and Roger Williams, *George Fox Digg'd out of his Burrovves* (Boston 1676), pp. 1-4, 25, 39, 138-39, etc.

[72]*Quakerism a New Nick-Name for Old Christianity* (London 1672), p. 11 in particular

[73]*Primitive Christianity* (London 1696), pp. 1-4, 50

[74]*A Brief Account of the Rise and Progress of the People called Quakers*, 5th edition (London 1748), p. 48

[75]*An Epistle containing a Salutation to all Faithful Friends* (London 1682), p. 2; and *An Epistle of Farewell* (London 1699), p. 5

[76]*A Divine and Supernatural Light* (Boston posth., n. d.), pp. 7-9, 19

[77]*Some Considerations on the Keeping of Negroes* (Philadelphia 1754), p. 2

[78]Roy Harvey Pearce, ed., *Colonial American Writing*, Rinehart Editions (N.Y.: Rinehart 1950), pp. 484-89

[79]*Records of the Court of Assistants of the Colony of the Massachusetts Bay 1630-1692* (Boston 1928), III, 110

[80]*An Epistle containing a Salutation*, p. 3. See also *A Brief Examination and State of Liberty Spiritual* (London 1681), preface; etc.

[81]Baillie, *A Dissvasive from the Errours of the Time* (London 1645) and *Anabaptism, the Trve Fovntaine of Independency, Browinisme, etc.* (London 1647); Edwards, *Gangraena* (London 1646); Pagitt, *Heresiography*, 3rd edition (London 1646); C. G. Coulton, *Medieval Panorama* (N.Y.: Macmillan 1938), pp. 521-22, citing Father Denifle; Trinterud, "The Origins of Puritanism," *Church History*, XX, 40-43, 48-55

[82]See Raymond Phineas Stearns. *The Strenuous Puritan: Hugh Peter 1598-1660* (Urbana: U. of Ill. 1954), pp. 53-90; Champlin Burrage, *The Early English Dissenters in the Light of Recent Research (1550-1641)*, 2 vols. (Cambridge: Cambridge U. 1912), I, 70-360; etc.

[83]See Henry Osborn Taylor, *Thought and Expression in the Sixteenth Century*, 2nd rev. edition (N.Y.: Macmillan 1930), II, 3-69, as well as Trinterud, *op. cit.*, etc.

[84]A. F. Scott Pearson, *Thomas Cartwright and Elizabethan Puritanism 1535-1603*

(Cambridge, Eng.: Cambridge U. 1925), pp. 47-57; M. M. Knappen, *Tudor Puritanism: a Chapter in the History of Idealism* (Chicago: U. of Chicago 1938), pp. 232-82

85*The New England Mind: the Seventeenth Century*, pp. 116-20, 146-50, 178; Burrage, I, 73-80; Stearns, *The Strenuous Puritan*, p. 19; Trinterud, *op. cit.;* etc.

86*History of Political Theory* (N.Y.: Holt 1937), pp. 377-78 *ff.*

87*The Accomplished Singer* (Boston 1721), p. 22

88Julius Freidrich Sachse, *The Music of the Ephrata Cloister* (Lancaster, Pa. 1903), pp. 90-91

89Tr. Christopher Witt, who joined Kelpius's brotherhood in 1704; Pa. Soc. Col. Dames of America, *Church Music and Musical Life in Pennsylvania in the Eighteenth Century*, 4 vols. (Philadelphia 1926-38), fac. reproduction of the hymnbook, I, 67, 85

90Adelaide L. Fries, *Funeral Chorals of Unitas Fratrum or Moravian Church* (Winston-Salem 1905), p. 6; the verse tr. F. W. Detterer

91T. M. Harris, "Chronological and Topographical Account of Dorchester," 1 MHS *Colls.*, IX, 156-58

92Samuel A. Harrison, *Wenlock Christison, and the Early Friends in Talbot County, Maryland* (Baltimore: Md. HS Fund Pubs. #9-13 [Mar. 1874] 1878), pp. 50-58

93Ian Charles Cargill Graham, *Colonists from Scotland* (Ithaca: Cornell U.-Am. Hist. Assoc. 1956), pp. 19-20. In 1825, incidentally, a book of devotionals by a Mrs. Taylor of "Ongar" was published in New York: *The Itinerary of a Traveller in the Wilderness. Addressed to Those who are performing the Same Journey.*

94Anonymous, *An Account of the Present State and Government of Virginia* [c. 1696-98], 1 MHS *Colls.*, V, 162

95*Notes on the State of Virginia* (Paris 1784), p. 289

96William Billings, *The Suffolk Harmony* (Boston 1786), pp. 33-34

97George Pullen Jackson, "Early American Religious Folk Songs," Mus. Teachers Nat'l Assoc. *Procs.* for 1934 (Oberlin 1935), pp. 78-79, and *White and Negro Spirituals* (N.Y.: Augustin 1943)

98G.F. & N.B., preface to Hugh Peter, *A Dying Fathers Last Legacy to an Onely Child* (London 1661)

99Peter, *ibid.*, pp. 87, 88

100Faust and Johnson, *Jonathan Edwards*, p. 61

101Cotton Mather, *Magnalia Christi Americana*, 2 vols. (Hartford 1820), Bk. III, appendix, I, 303, 314

102*The Sovles Preparation for Christ* (London 1632), pp. 4, 182

103*Experiments of Spiritual Health*, p. 31

104*Insanabilia. An Essay upon Incurables* (Boston 1714), p. 9

105*Ibid.*, 10

106Quoted in Mather, *Magnalia* (1820), I, 311

107*A Serious Exhortation to the Present and Succeeding Generations in New-England* (Cambridge 1672), pp. 9, 25, 28, 30

108To Robert Cushman (9 June 1625), *Letter Book*, 1 MHS *Colls.*, III, 36

109*Of Plimmoth Plantation*, pp. 397, 503

110*A Trve and Short Declaration* (Middelburg c. 1583), fac. in Burrage, *Early English Dissenters*, I, between pp. 180 & 181

111*General Observations for the Plantation of New-England* (c. Aug. 1629), "Draft C," *Winthrop Papers*, II, 114. See Christopher Hill, "Recent Interpretations of the Civil War," in *Puritanism and Revolution* (London: Secker & Warburg 1958), pp. 3-31.

112*Winthrop Papers*, II, 114

113Joseph H. Twichell, ed., *Some old Puritan Love-Letters* (N.Y. 1893), pp. 100, 105

114*A Sermon preached at Plimmoth in Nevv-England December 9. 1621* (London 1622), Epistle dedicatory

115*The Danger of Desertion: or a Farvvell Sermon* (London 1641), pp. 5, 15, 20

116*The Examination of Mrs. Ann Hutchinson at the Court at Newton*, in Thomas Hutchinson, *History of the Colony and Province of Massachusetts-Bay*, ed. Lawrence Shaw Mayo, 3 vols. (Cambridge: Harvard U. 1936), II, appendix, p. 385

117*A Serious Exhortation*, p. 7

118*Ibid.*, preface p. [ii]

119*Autobiography* (msc.c. 1647) [photostat in Widener], unnumbered pp. in back

120*Magnalia* (1702), VII, 20

[121]*An Essay for the Recording of Illustrious Providences* (Boston 1684; reprint London 1856 as *Remarkable Providences*), p. 175

[122]*Kometographia* (Boston 1683), pp. 1-2, 13, 132, 133, 141-42. See also his *Heavens Alarm to the World* (Boston 1681) and *Angelographia* (Boston 1696).

[123]To Daniel Abbot (15 Jan. 1681), *Letters*, ed. John R. Bartlett, Narr. Club *Pubs.*, VI (Providence 1874), pp. 402-03

[124]*Diary of Samuel Sewall*, I: 5 MHS *Colls.*, V, 402 (Mon. Apr. 29)

[125]*The Wonders of the Invisible World* (Boston 1693; reprint London 1862), pp. 3, 4-5, 13-15

[126]*Autobiography* (msc. transcription by A. P. Marvin 1881, of orig. msc. Am. Antiq. Soc.), p. 112, under the year 1687

[127]*Life of Edwards*, pp. 44-45

[128]*Experiments of Spiritual Health*, p. 3; *The Bloody Tenent Yet More Bloody* (London 1652), p. 302

[129]Memorandum in a diary of John Baily, quoted in Cotton Mather, *A Good Man making a Good End*, p. 56

[130]*The Blessed Hope, and the Glorious Appearing of the Great God our Saviour* (Boston 1701), pp. 42-43

[131]Quoted in Thomas James Holmes, *Increase Mather: a Bibliography of his Works*, 2 vols. (Cleveland 1931), I, 24-26

[132]*Solemn Advice* (Boston 1695), pp. 8-9, 14-16, 24-27, 65

[133]*A Testimony against Several Prophane and Superstitious Customs* (London 1687), p. A2, Cf. Cotton Mather, *Advice from the Watch Tower. In a Testimony against Evil Customes* (Boston 1713)

[134]*An Earnest Exhortation to the Inhabitants of New-England* (Boston 1676), pp. 6-7, 9, 26. Cf. his *The Day of Trouble is Near* (Cambridge 1674); *Pray for the Rising Generation* (Cambridge 1678); *Ichabod. Or, a Discourse, shewing what Cause there is to Fear that the Glory of the Lord, is departing from New-England* (Boston 1702); and *Burnings Bewailed* (Boston 1711); etc.

[135]*Wo to Drunkards* (Cambridge 1673), p. 29. Cf. such other of his works as *The Doctrine of Divine Providence* (Boston 1684), pp. 98-99; also Covey, "Puritan Morals," in Vergilius Ferm, ed., *Encyclopedia of Morals* (N.Y.: Philosophical Library 1956), pp. 446-59

[136]Quoted in Haller, *Rise of Puritanism*, p. 145

[137]"Meditations and Spiritual Experiences," p. 67 (24 Nov. 1641)

[138]Quoted in Cotton Mather, *A Good Man making a Good End*, pp. 49, 51

[139]Dwight, *Life of President Edwards*, p. 105

[140]*A Guide to Christ* (Boston 1714), pp. 10-11

[141]J. Franklin Jameson, ed. (orig. 1654), Orig. Narrs. series (N.Y.: Scribner's 1910), p. 135

[142]*Winthrop Papers*, I, 160

[143]*Meditations Divine and Morall*, pp. 51, 54, 55-59

[144]John Harvard Ellis, ed., *The Works of Anne Bradstreet in Prose and Verse* (N.Y.: Peter Smith 1932; reprint of 1867 edition), p. 404

[145]*Autobiography*, pp. 28-29

[146]*An Earnest Exhortation*, p. 19

[147]*Diary of Samuel Sewall*, III: 5 MHS *Colls.*, VII, 326. This was Tues. 30 Jul. 1723; Increase died Fri. Aug. 23 following.

[148]*Parentator* (Boston 1724), pp. 207-08

[149]*Diary*, II: 7 MHS *Colls.*, VIII, 3

[150]*The Life of the Very Reverend and Learned Cotton Mather* (Boston 1729), p. 159

[151]*Corderius Americanus. A Discourse on the Good Education of Children* (Boston 1828), p. 16

[152]Ernest Caulfield, *Some Common Diseases of Colonial Children*, Col. Soc. Mass. *Pubs.*, XXXV, 4-65. Caulfield says diphtheria and dysentery outranked smallpox as a cause of death, that chickenpox and mumps were relatively harmless, and that whooping cough was regarded as a much milder disease than now. See also Caulfield's monograph on influenza in early New England: "The Pursuit of a Pestilence," Am. Antiq. Soc. *Procs.*, LX, 22 *ff.* (Margaret Winthrop and Thomas Hooker seem to have died in a 'flu epidemic.) For statistics on smallpox in Boston, see T. P., "A

Topographical and Historical Description of Boston, 1794," 1 MHS *Colls.*, III, 292-93, and "Account of Burials and Baptisms in Boston, from the Year 1701 to 1774," 1 MHS *Colls.*, IV, 213-16.

153*Diary*, II, 187, 236, 260-262. The most poignant passages in Judge Sewall's *Diary* also concern the death, or fear of death, of his children.

154*Diary* (Mather's), *ibid.*, 267

155*Ibid.*, 753. Cf. Winthrop's reaction to the drowning of his wayward son Henry.

156Samuel A. Green, ed., *Diary by Increase Mather, March, 1675-December, 1676. Together with Extracts from Another Diary by him, 1674-1687* (Cambridge 1900; reprint from MHS *Procs.*) pp. 6-8

157Thomas H. Johnson, "Edward Taylor: a Puritan Sacred Poet," *N. Eng. Quarterly*, X, 293

158*Ibid.*, 307; "Meditation One" of Taylor's *Sacramental Meditations* (Westfield 23 Jul. 1682)

159*Magnalia* (1702), p.

160Hopkins, *Life of Edwards*, p. 27

161*The Reflexion*, in Johnson, "Edward Taylor," p. 310

162*Cotton Mather, the Puritan Priest* (Cambridge: Harvard U. 1926), pp. 183, 221

163*A Sketch of Eminent Men in New-England* (6 May 1768), 1 MHS *Colls.*, X, 156. Cf. the glowing remarks on Mather by the Marblehead minister, John Barnard (16 Oct. 1767), *ibid.*, p. 168

164*Paterna* (msc. in Alderman Library), pp. 4-6

165*Manly Christianity* (London 1711), p. 16

166*Dairy*, I: 7 MHS *Colls.*, VII, 148

167*Ibid.*, 163

168*Ibid.*, 456-57 (Jan. 1703)

169*Ibid.*, 457

170*Bonifacius. An Essay upon the Good, that is to be devised and designed, by those who desire to answer the Great End of Life, and to Do Good while they live* (Boston 1710), pp. ix-x, 183, 193. The text proper following the Preface is headed "Essays to Do Good," and subsequent editions of the book bore this title on the title page in place of the original title. Although my quotations come from the first edition, I refer to the book by its better-known name.

171Increase Mather, *Autobiography*, p. 175 (a passage repeated in Cotton Mather's *Parentator*); Increase, *Cases of Conscience* (Boston 1693), esp. pp. 1, 67, and appended "The Return of Several Ministers . . . ," III & IV; Thomas J. Holmes, *Cotton Mather: a Bibliography of his Works*, 3 vols. (Cambridge: Harvard U. 1940), III, 920, 1249, 1252, 1258-60; Holmes, *Increase Mather*, I, 123, 124-27, 129-33. Perry Miller, *The New England Mind from Colony to Province* (Cambridge: Harvard U. 1953), p. 493, calls attention to Holmes's analytical feat recorded in the bibliographies cited above.

172Miller, *Colony to Province*, pp. 410-11, 416, 419, 476

173*The Christian Philosopher* (London 1721), pp. 1, 2

174*Biblia Americana* (msc. in MHS, microfilm via Recordak Corp.), I, Introduction, & text proper: pp. [1], [24], [29-30], [35-44]; appendix to *Acts*; V, "An Essay"

175*Diary*, II, 786

176*The Comfortable Chambers Opened and Visited*, p. 3

177Charles Sanford, "An American Pilgrim's Progress," in *Benjamin Franklin and the American Character*, Probs. in Am. Civ. series (N.Y.: Heath 1955), pp. 71-73

178"Articles of Belief and Acts of Religion," *Works*, ed. Bigelow, I, 323

179*Bonifacius*, pp. 28-29

180Quoted by George Burder in preface to *Essays to Do Good* (Portsmouth, Eng. 1824), pp. 6-7

181*Letter-Book of Samuel Sewall*, 6 MHS *Colls.*, I, 407

182*Works*, ed. C. F. Adams, I, 664; from *The Boston Patriot* (15 May 1811)

183*Death Made Easie & Happy*, p. 23

184*The Great Chain of Being* (Cambridge: Harvard U. 1950; lectures orig. given 1933). John Adams restates the doctrine of the great chain of being in his *Discourses on Davila* (Boston 1805; first pub. as newspaper article 1790), p. 20. Winthrop employs it, though not by name, in *A Modell of Christian Charity* (1630), *Winthrop Papers*,

II, 282-83.

[185]Oscar Handlin reviews these relationships in the fall semester of his seminal history course, *The Immigrant*, at Harvard.

[186]Quoted in Ola Elizabeth Winslow, *Jonathan Edwards* (N.Y.: Macmillan 1940), p. 224

[187]*Life of Edwards*, p. 56

[188]*Life of President Edwards*, p. 429

[189]Caulfield, *Some Common Diseases of Colonial Children*, pp. 15-17

[190]Mellen Chamberlain, *A Documentary History of Chelsea*, 2 vols. (Boston 1908), II, 206-13. Cf. Wise, *Churches Quarrel Espoused*, 2nd edition (Boston 1715), pp. 9, 27, 116

[191]"Solomon Stoddard, 1643-1729," *Harvard Theol. Rev.*, XXXIV, 311

[192]See Increase, *A Narrative of the Miseries of New-England, by Reason of an Arbitrary Government Erected there* (London? 1688); the scorching letters of Increase and Cotton to Dudley (20 Jan. 1708), 1 MHS *Colls.*, III, 126-28; etc.

[193]Quoted in Miller, "Solomon Stoddard," p. 305

[194]John Cotton, *The Way of the Churches of Christ in New-England* (London 1645), p. 100

[195]*Ichabod*, p. 40

[196]*Autobiography*, p. 114

[197]*An Humble Inquiry into the Rules of the Word of God, concerning the Qualifications Requisite to a Compleat Standing and Full Communion in the Visible Christian Church* (Boston 1749), p. ii, quoting Stoddard's preface to *Appeal to the Learned*

[198]*Ibid.*, iii, iv

[199]*Ibid.*, 28-29

[200]*God Glorified in the Work of Redemption, by the Greatness of Man's Dependance upon Him, in the Whole of it* (Boston 1731), pp. 21-24

[201]*Life of President Edwards*, p. 118

[202]*God Glorified in the Work of Redemption*, pp. 1-2. See also *Miscellaneous Remarks on Important Doctrines*, in *Works*, ed. Dwight, VII, 413, 484, 571-72; Vincent Tomas, "The Modernity of Jonathan Edwards," *N. Eng. Quarterly*, XXV, 70-84; Clarence H. Faust, "Jonathan Edwards as a Scientist," *Am. Lit.*, I, 393-404; Carl van Doren, ed., *Benjamin Franklin and Jonathan Edwards* (N.Y.: Scribner's 1920), pp. x-xxxiv; and John P. R. Budlong, *Jonathan Edwards and the 'Great Awakening'* (msc. honors thesis, Harvard 1948), p. 45

[203]*Personal Narrative*, in Hopkins, *Life of Edwards* (where it was first published), p. 25

[204]*An Unpublished Essay . . . on the Trinity*, ed. George P. Fisher (N.Y.: Scribner's 1903), p. 95

[205]*A Treatise concerning Religious Affections* (Boston 1746), p. 13

[206]*Treatise on Grace*, in *Selections from the Unpublished Writings of Jonathan Edwards, of America*, ed. Alexander B. Grosart (Edinburgh 1865), p. 33. See also *Concerning the End for which God created the World*, in *Two Dissertations* (Boston 1767), pp. 109-113; and Thomas A. Schafer, "Jonathan Edwards and Justification by Faith," *Church History*, XX, 60-61.

[207]Sermon on *Hosea* 5. 15, in *Works*, ed. Dwight, VIII, 45

[208]*All the Living Must Surely Die, and Go to Judgment* (New London 1732), p. 1

[209]*Burnings Bewailed*, p. 9

[210]*Magnalia* (1702), V, pt. I, p. 3; *A Platform of Church-Discipline* (London 1653), pp. 1, 2

[211]*The Sovles Hvmiliation* (London 1638), pp. 98-100

[212]*Magnalia* (Hartford 1820), p. 250

[213]*The Marrow of Sacred Divinity* (London 1642), p. 177

[214]*Sermons of Master John Caluin, vpon the Booke of Iob*, tr. Arthur Golding (London 1574), pp. 1, 825. See also Sermon on 1 *Timothy*, 3.16, in *A Selection of the Most Celebrated Sermons*, p. 33; etc.

[215]*Sermons of M. Iohn Caluine vpon the Epistle of Saincte Paule to the Galatians* (London 1574), pp. 1, 229. Innumerable other instances could be cited from sermons of Calvin translated into English up through 1620, which were easily available to the first generation of American Puritans in their formative years, e.g. *Two and Twentie Sermons of Maister Iohn Caluin . . . . [on] the Hundredth and Nineteenth Psalme*, tr. Thomas Stocker (London 1580), pp. 45-63; and the most monumental of all, *Sermons of M. John Caluin; vpon the X. Commandements of the Lawe*, tr.

John Harmar (London 1581), pp. 8-14 *ad inf.*

216Calvin and Covenant Theology," *Church History*, XXV, 142. *Cf.* Perry Miller, "The Marrow of Puritan Divinity," *Col. Soi. Mass. Pubs.*, XXXII (Feb. 1935), pp. 247-300

217James Savage, ed., *The History of New England from 1630 to 1649, by John Winthrop*, new edition, 2 vols. (Boston 1853), I, 339-40

218*The Distinguishing Marks of a Work of the Spirit of God* (Boston 1741), p. 31

219*An Humble Inquiry*, pp. 42-43

220George Pierce Clark, ed., "An Unpublished Letter by Jonathan Edwards" (Northampton 7 May 1750), *N. Eng. Quarterly*, XXIX, 231

221*Ibid.*, and *Some Thoughts concerning the Present Revival of Religion in New-England* (Boston 1743), preface, iii

222*Hades Look'd Into* (Boston 1717), p. 20

223"Introduction," Faust and Johnson, *Jonathan Edwards*, p. lxxiv

224Edwards to a Boston clergyman [Colman?] (12 Dec. 1743), in Dwight, *Life of President Edwards*, p. 160

225*Eleutheria* (London 1698), subtitle

226*Some Thoughts concerning the Present Revival*, p. 55

227*Ibid.*, 5

228Msc. sermon in *Cole Papers*, Amherst Hist. Coll., Morgan Library, pp. 1, 27

229*Words*, ed. Dwight, I, 538

230*Distinguishing Marks*, pp. 37-38

231Thomas Prince, msc. note appended to Shepard's msc. *Autobiography*. Prince is one of those who preserves the tradition of Edwards's style of preaching at first hand, in *An Account of the Revival of Religion in Boston, in the Years 1740-1-2-3* (Boston 1823), p. 13. See Perry Miller, *Orthodoxy in Massachusetts 1630-1650, a Genetic Study* (Cambridge: Harvard U. 1933), pp. 204, 254-58, etc.

232*The Sincere Convert; discovering the Small Number of True Believers, and the Great Difficulty of Saving Conversion* (London 1672), pp. 62-63. *Cf.* Hooker, *The Sovles Preparation for Christ* (London 1634), pp. 13-14

233*The Day of Trouble is Near*, p. [i]

234*Renewal of Covenant the Great Day Incumbent on Decaying or Distressed Churches* (Boston 1677). The preface, dated May 22, in particular reaffirms the covenant doctrine of the first generation. See also *A Discourse concerning the Danger of Apostacy* [election sermon 23 May 1677] (Boston 1685), pp. 76-78, 87-90.

235"Christians ought to work out their own Salvation, and that with Fear and Trembling," in *Some Important Truths about Conversion*, 2nd edition (London 1674; reprint Boston 1721), pp. 225, 229

236*Wo to Drunkards*, p. 33

237*A Guide to Christ*, p. 7. See also Calvin, *Sermons vpon . . . Galatians*, p. 158

238*Enthusiasm Described and Caution'd Against* (Boston 1742), p. 3 & *passim; Seasonable Thoughts on the State of Religion in New-England* (Boston 1743), *passim* & particularly the 30-page preface retracing the Antinomian experience of more than 100 years before

239*Distinguishing Marks*, pp. 98-99

240*A Faithful Advice . . . relating to the Dangers that may arise from Imposters pretending to be Ministers* (Boston 1699), in *Magnalia* (1702), VII, 31

241[Chauncy], *Salvation for All Men* (Boston 1782), esp. the preface, dated Aug. 1782 and signed "T.W."; Samuel Mather, *All Men Will Not be Saved Forever*, 2nd edition (Boston 1783); Jonathan Edwards Jr., *The Salvation of All Men Strictly Examined* (New-Haven 1790), preface (dated 29 June 1789), p. iii, *passim*

242*Jonathan Edwards* (N.Y.: Sloane 1949) p. 147. *Cf.* Miller's "Marrow of Puritan Divinity," *op. cit.*

243*Sinners in the Hands of an Angry God, a Sermon preached at Enfield, July 8th. 1741*, 3rd edition (Boston 1772), pp. 7, 13-14, 16, 27

244Quoted in Raymond P. Stearns, "Assessing the New England Mind," *Church History*, X, 253. See Thomas Shepard, *The Clear Sun-Shine of Gospel breaking forth upon the Indians in New-England* (London 1648), in *Tracts relating to the Attempts to convert to Christianity the Indians of New England*, 3 MHS Colls., IV, 55-56

245*Two Discourses* (Boston 1716), p. 3

[246]Whitefield, *Free Grace Indeed!* (Boston 1741), pp. 3 & (quoting Wesley) 6, 21

[247]*A Continuation* [the 6th] *of the Reverend Mr. Whitefield's Journal . . . The Seventh Journal* (London 1741), pp. 37, 45-47

[248]*A Careful and Strict Enquiry into the Modern Prevailing Notions of that Freedom of Will, which is supposed to be Essential to Moral Agency, Vertue and Vice, Reward and Punishment, Praise and Blame* (Boston 1754), pp. 12, 32. See Conrad Wright, "Edwards and the Arminians on the Freedom of the Will," *Harvard Theol. Rev.*, XXV, 241-61; Thomas A. Schafer, "Jonathan Edwards and Justification by Faith," 56-64, 67, Frederic I. Carpenter, "The Radicalism of Jonathan Edwards," *N. Eng. Quarterly*; IV, 634-43; Tomas, "The Modernity of Jonathan Edwards," pp. 75-76 & *passim*; Vergilius Ferm, ed., *Puritan Sage: Collected Writings of Jonathan Edwards* (N.Y.: Library Pubs. 1953), pp. xv-xix; Faust, "Introduction," Faust and Johnson, *Jonathan Edwards*, pp. xxiv-lxxiv; occasional clarifying notes in Edwards's *Miscellanies*, in Harvey G. Townsend, *The Philosophy of Jonathan Edwards from his Private Notebooks* (Eugene, Ore.: Oregon U. 1955), p. 209 & *passim*; Winslow, *Jonathan Edwards*, pp. 299-304; and Paul Ramsey, ed., Edwards, *Freedom of the Will* (New Haven: Yale U. 1957), pp. 8-118.

[249]*Treatise on Grace*, pp. 25, 28

[250]*Miscellaneous Remarks on Important Doctrines*, in *Works*, ed. Dwight, VII, 484, 572; see also p. 413, etc.

[251]"The Nature of True Virtue," in *Two Dissertations*, pp. 117-18, 123

[252]*Treatise concerning Religious Affections*, pp. 8-9 (drawn up in 1746 from sermons preached probably in 1742-43)

[253]Hopkins, *Life of Edwards*, pp. 53-55; Dwight, *Life of President Edwards*, pp. 428-34; Winslow, *Jonathan Edwards*, pp. 216-31. See also Joseph Tracy, *The Great Awakening* (Boston 1842).

[254]To the Rev. James Robe, of Kilsyth; and to the Rev. Thomas Gillespie, of Carnock, quoted in Dwight, *Life of President Edwards*, pp. 279, 413

[255]Quoted in Winslow, *Jonathan Edwards*, p. 224

[256]Lawrence Gene Lavengood, *The Great Awakening and New England Society* (msc. doctoral diss. U. of Chicago 1953), pp. 16, 314 *ff*. My treatment of Edwards and the Great Awakening has been influenced throughout by this important study.

[257]Edwards, *A Faithful Narrative of the Surprizing Work of God*, p. 9; Mather, *A Midnight Cry* (Boston 1692), p. 61, etc.

[258]*A Farewell-Sermon preached at the First Precinct in Northampton, after the People's Publick Rejection of their Minister . . . on June 22. 1750* (Boston 1751), pp. 2-22 & *passim*.

[259]Whitefield, *Seventh Journal*, p. 7

[260]*Western Massachusetts in the Revolution* (Providence: Brown U. 1954), chaps. II-IV

[261]*A Strong Rod Broken and Withered* [funeral sermon for John Stoddard 26 June 1748] (Boston 1748)

[262]John Bishop to Increase Mather (18 Oct. 1687), 4 MHS *Colls.*, VIII, 315

[263]See Covey, "Did Puritanism or the Frontier Cause the Decline of Colonial Music?" *Journ. of Research in Mus. Ed.* (summer 1958), pp. 68-78

[264]*The Peril of the Times Displayed* (Boston 1700), To the Reader, p. 4

[265]*Ibid.*, 97, 113-15, 138

[266]"Take orders" is Harry A. Wolfson's language quoted by Tomas, "The Modernity of Jonathan Edwards," p. 70

[267]Quoted in Thomas Herbert Johnson, *Jonathan Edwards as a Man of Letters* (msc. doctoral diss. Harvard 1932), pp. 281-82

[268]Perry Miller, ed., *Images or Shadows of Divine Things* (New Haven: Yale U. 1948), pp. 136-37

[269]William H. Herndon and Jesse W. Weik, *Abraham Lincoln*, 2 vols. (N.Y. & London: Appleton 1928), I, 10; II, 297

[270]*Ibid.*, II, 194-95

[271]Paul M. Angle, ed., *The Lincoln Reader* (New Brunswick: Rutgers U. 1947), pp. 523-24, from Seward's *Reminiscences of a War-Time Statesman and Diplomat* (N.Y.: Putnam 1916). The previous dream: *ibid.*, 521, from Ward Hill Lamon, *Recollections of Lincoln* (1895)

[272]Richard Chase, *Emily Dickinson* (N.Y.: Sloane 1951), pp. 165, 172, 182

[273]"The Ship of Death," in *D. H. Lawrence: Selected Poems* (N.Y.: New Directions 1947), pp. 140, 144

[274]*Magnalia* (1820), I, 304

[275]*A Dying Fathers Last Legacy*, pp. 89-90

[276]"On the sudden Death of Messieurs George and Nathan Howell, the only Children of Madam Sewall, who were lost as they were skating on the Ice, January 8th, 1727, 8," *Poems on Several Occasions*, pp. 81-82